D0282664

Jean-Paul Sartre:

PHILOSOPHER WITHOUT FAITH

Jean-Paul Sartre:

PHILOSOPHER WITHOUT FAITH

By RENÉ MARILL-ALBÉRÈS

THE PHILOSOPHICAL LIBRARY
New York

Translated from the original French by Wade Baskin

Library of Congress Catalog Card Number: 60-15950

Manufactured in the United States of Ameria.

CONTENTS

Special thanks are due to Mr. Raymond Piller, who not only compiled the list of English titles included in the appended bibliography but also made available to me a number of important works by and about Sartre. Though I have profited in many instances by consulting the English works cited, all translations of quotations from Sartre's writings are my own.

WADE BASKIN

Jean-Paul Sartre:

PHILOSOPHER WITHOUT FAITH

I. SYSTEM AND SCOPE

A. POINTS OF DEPARTURE

The painstaking analysis and logical systematization of man's solitude, freedom, and responsibility, and the desire to probe the consequences of man's independence and of his ultimate responsibility to himself—such are apparently the touchstones of the works which appeared between 1938 and 1946 and which made Jean-Paul Sartre a writer renowned throughout the world.

Sartre's views are not new to our age. It may well be that the salient characteristic of the twentieth century is the absence of a rigorous doctrine to explain and direct human life. Horror in the face of convention and of the revelation of man's nakedness is found at the dawn of the century in Péguy as well as in Gide and Unamuno, and the human drama that Malraux and Camus subsequently lived through is also that of man confronted by his destiny.

Nor is such an attitude essentially atheistic. To Bernanos also, man is free and responsible, and alone in the dark. The idea that the paths of our lives are not marked out but depend solely on us, that "everything must forever be begun anew,"[1] that there are no rules to govern our conduct and no systems to bring us stability and peace of mind, is in point of fact the hallmark of the literature of our time; and Christianity, through its most convincing and effective writers, views life not as an established order but as an adventure.

The great doctrine of Progress which caught up in its wake such men as Lamartine and Hugo has lost its appeal. The harmonious syntheses of Classicism and the great systems of the Enlightenment belong to the past.

The result is that man, cut off from the support of ready-made doctrines in which he no longer believes, is aware of his *solitude*. And in his loneliness his anxiety mounts as he becomes aware of his freedom and his *responsibility*. At the heart of the works of Bernanos, Malraux, Graham Greene, and Camus is the apparently contradictory and yet *ineluctable relation of solitude to responsibility*. The paradoxical relation has been labeled "the tragic element," "anguish," "fate," and even "absurdity." Man no longer believes in pat explanations and conventional, expedient rules for living, and yet the absence of external props and restraints does not eliminate his responsibility. On the contrary, recognition of his responsibility increases his anguish, with the result that the problem has finally invaded all literature and given it what is carelessly called a "metaphysical" aspect. This aspect is in fact *moral*.

The moral problem is at the heart not only of Sartre's writings but also of those of his predecessors and contemporaries.

His originality, however, resides in the fact that he treats the problem *systematically* and philosophically. The most original characteristic of Sartre's work seems at first glance to be the formulation in philosophical terms, and therefore the systematic formulation (to the extent that it is reduced to methodical postulates) of the great moral problem of the twentieth century: the anguish brought about by man's responsibility in the absence of any restraint on the exercise of his responsibility.

Man can not simply enjoy the existing world but must take a definite stand. This Sartre discovered and expressed in his most famous works, produced between 1938 and 1946, between *Nausea* and *Roads to Freedom*. It is the same necessity to act in the face of the world and the situations which it provides for us and imposes on us that Sartre has been interpreting since 1946 *while changing from a psychological and moralistic writer to a political and social analyst*. But this second period is also characterized by the formation of a school and by the publishing and editing of a monthly journal, *Les Temps Modernes*. If Sartre's writings and pattern of living have taken a new tack since 1946, and if he has tended to become a cartoonist rather than a writer, the change was first imposed by his work as a moralist and by his talent as an artist.

Until 1946 Sartre's writings, though designed to serve as concrete illustrations of his philosophical system, are also prime examples of his art. His novels have a life and an atmosphere of their own; they have a literary existence which at first fails even to suggest that they illustrate a doctrine. *Nausea* at first seems to be an account of the boredom and obsessions of an isolated, disabused celibate living in a little town he despises. Certain episodes in *The Wall* and in *Intimacy* at first seem to be obliging descriptions of obscene and frivolous beings. The first volumes of *Roads to Freedom* at first seem to be a sympathetic satire on weary Frenchmen who in 1938 are waiting in the Parisian bistros for the war to begin.

And certainly it is tempting to consider separately the fictional world that emerges in his early works, for it has a certain unity: trite urban scenes with nothing at the end of the avenues; ineffective but intelligent, and not wholly worthless characters without horizons and with stunted lives, always seen outside their working hours and often hard put to kill time. They are in general the human beings most frequently seen on the sidewalk or at the counter in a café but never in a group, whether in church, in the country, in the mountains, or in a foreign land; in short, the opposite of boy scouts, and prime examples of men who might be defined according to existential psychoanalysis by *their fear of being dupes*. As Sartre himself puts it:

> "Well, my friend," she said, "your lucidity always makes me laugh. You are so scared that you would give up the best deal in the world rather than risk self-deception."
>
> "Yes, of course you're right," said Mathieu. "That's what I've been telling you all along." [2]

Sartre has been censured for depicting such situations, and sometimes a pharisaical element has entered into the criticism. But these situations are chosen for the very reason that they epitomize the rejection of the ineluctable responsibility which is imposed on man and which Camus and Malraux bring to the fore with more restrained lyricism.

6

Mathieu in *Roads to Freedom* is indeed a man who eludes his responsibility. But *it is precisely by refusing to assume it that he affirms it and proves its existence*. It is through a sort of reduction to the absurd that Sartre tries to focus attention on human responsibility in beings who reject it. Those who accept it prove nothing; they only affirm their belief in their destiny. Sartre pretends to *prove* the existence of human responsibility by pointing up its absence or its suppression among those who slight it. That he may show partiality and undue concern in depicting inaction is something else, and this brings up the eternal problem of the writer who in depicting Evil and lust so as to make them abhorrent may be a victim of his own game. This criticism has actually been directed against both Racine and Mauriac.

* * *

Man's moral solitude, which brings into focus his inevitable responsibility, is not the sole concern of other writers who have examined and protested man's fate. In Camus there is a sort of cosmic, Mediterranean brotherhood which reasserts the mating of man and the world; in Malraux, a dialog with eternity; and in Bernanos, of course, an almost carnal union between God and Satan. Still, for these three writers the central problem is the same as for Sartre, man's responsibility in the face of his destiny.

But one can find in Sartre no cosmic vision, no suggestion of the human adventure, and of course no faith. Man is imprisoned in the human consciousness, alienated from the earth, landscapes, the cosmos. Everything that can bring about a harmoni-

7

ous relation is obviously revealed through man's consciousness; since this fact serves as his philosophical point of departure, Sartre limits himself to describing the human consciousness. Fugitive landscapes appear as an object of consciousness; no animistic illusion gives them life. God himself can be discussed in this life only as an object of human consciousness, and since it can not wholly conceive of Him and define Him, Sartre concludes that He does not exist. That is why *his universe is limited to consciousness.*

His fictional world is narrow and restricted like that of novelists and classic dramatists concerned solely with the study of the emotions; that is why it is both deadening and dense.

In this sense Sartre allies himself with moralists and is a moralist, that is, a writer who makes it his *sole task to observe, describe, and if need be to judge human conduct.* He has no concern and apparently not even any love for anything other than man—neither nature nor animals nor physical life nor the universe. His only universe is man, and even more specifically the conscious, adult man inured to life and capable of formulating its problems; the child who appears in *Roads to Freedom*[3] does not belong to his universe, and when he forces himself into it, Mathieu is surprised:

> Little Pablo looked at him. There he stood, tiny and puzzled; but behind the dull humors that filled his sockets lurked a greedy little consciousness.
>
> "You know what I dreamed?" asked Pablo.
> "What?"

"I dreamed that I was a feather."
"That figures," Mathieu thought.[4]

Sartre's vision is limited to man, and to man
wrapped up in his own human problems. He does
not try to relate man to other, more imposing realities that surround him, as do Giraudoux, Claudel,
and Malraux with their cosmic vision. In his view
man is independent, "given"; man is of interest to
him only when separated from other things, real or
hypothetical, through philosophical reflection. In
the strictly human domain which he has appropri-
ated, Sartre refuses to give in to certain temptations,
such as the cultivation of the picturesque side of
people or a predilection for romantic adventures.
There are few events in the stories that he relates,
and these events are always *psychological and moral
events.*

That is why, however novel his style may have
appeared when given the public's stamp of approval,
he has done nothing more than adopt the attitude
and angle of vision of the French moralists. He has
less gentleness and breadth than Montaigne, less
charm than La Bruyère, less concern for grandeur
that Stendhal, and perhaps much less than La Rochefoucauld or Pascal. Like La Rochefoucauld, he analyzes human conduct in order to fashion a system
for judging it. Like Pascal he insists on the *justification or nonjustification of acts and poses the
essential problem of their value* when judged in
terms of man's fate rigidly and harshly defined.

Nevertheless, there is no contradiction in the fact
that a "moralist" can be accused of "immorality."
Observing, describing, and passing judgment on man

9

do not necessarily imply judging him according to criteria labeled "moral" by society. As a matter of fact, the charge of immorality that has frequently been made against Sartre can be understood only in the light of the three premises on which it is grounded.

First, to the extent that he observes and analyzes man, Sartre gives an account of the whole human reality and even of the part that modesty conceals. This realism may be shocking, but Sartre's defense is that he is exercising his privilege as a scientific observer and that as a physician of the soul he is compelled to overlook nothing and to surprise man in every possible posture in his search for absolute truth. But beyond this, it has been charged that in his concern for openness and exactness he not only seeks to reveal man's abject wretchedness but also shows in certain scenes an obvious predilection for it. It is therefore charged that his immorality consists, not in depicting truth too audaciously, but in surrounding certain scenes with an affective halo which, even while leaving them with their unpleasant character, confers on them a dangerous power of fascination.

Finally, and most important, Sartre does not restrict himself to describing, he also acts as judge and seeks to suggest, perhaps not rules, but at least patterns of conduct, and may in this way establish moral criteria which are not those of the society of which he is a part and which will therefore judge him "immoral."

It is fitting to point out that the Roman Catholic Church has placed on the Index all of Sartre's works.

* * *

In sum, we must note that if Sartre's fictional universe has a certain literary coherence and personal atmosphere and is apparently self-explanatory, it is in fact the illustration of a theory and requires interpretation.

In this sense it can even be said that Sartre is an esoteric writer, for his novels and his characters have a general meaning as well as a hidden meaning. For those not versed in philosophy his characters acquire a certain meaning at first reading; but to get at the meaning which Sartre confers on them, it is necessary to *decipher them with the help of his philosophical works.*

Esoteric texts have an obvious meaning and a meaning known only to priests and initiates. Here, too, we are confronted by a work which, independently of the literary impression made by the first reading, has a hidden meaning accessible only to the initiates, to those schooled in philosophy. One of his most intelligent commentators, Francis Jeanson, makes an admission which will show many readers who were at first rebuffed that their reaction was also the initial reaction of Sartre's best disciple:

> We admit—and our admission is hardly painful—having reacted violently to each contact with Sartre's theory. Having approached it from the literary angle, we first experienced *something very close to disgust.* To be specific, we did not succeed in going beyond page 30 in *Roads of Freedom.* Then, impelled by a sort of quasi-professional necessity, we turned to his philosophical works: we discovered the magic of a mode of expression perfectly adapted to

11

theoretical perspectives. . . . Then we again read his short stories and novels, and saw the theatrical productions which were causing quite a stir. That was a decisive enlargement on our previous discovery; in short, his theory was revealed to us in its very movement; we experienced *its true dynamism and felt capable of extracting from it for ourselves something of practical value.*[5]

B. THE LAST WRITER OF THE THIRTIES AND THE FIRST WRITER OF THE FORTIES

In Sartre's first and perhaps greatest novel, *Nausea,* a man discovers in anguish that nothing in his life is motivated or justified, that still this gratuity does not deliver him from his freedom and from his responsibility, and that it is up to him and him alone to create justifications.

This exacting freedom, given to man in an existence wherein nothing is ready to receive him and help him, demands its due, and so long as it remains empty and in suspension, manifests itself in the form of uneasiness. It follows that it must be committed (*s'engager*).

But commitment, or the specific employment of freedom which constitutes our personality and our responsibility, is a late development in the life of Sartre. Prior to 1940 (or more exactly prior to 1943, since he published nothing between 1940 and

12

1943), *Nausea* and *The Wall,* as well as a few specialized philosophical works, are but the discovery of this freedom and its gratuitousness.

For Sartre was born almost at the turn of the century, on June 21, 1905, in Paris. It was during his childhood that he became acquainted with middle-class ostentation, genteel books, Barbedian bronze pieces on the mantel. At an early age he lost his father, a Polytechnician who died in Cochin-China, but his mother soon remarried a second Polytechnician, the director of the Chantiers Maritimes in La Rochelle. He was eleven when he went to La Rochelle, where he learned of the confidence of the middle class in its security, its duties, and especially its rights; later he was to satirize this bourgeois smugness in *Nausea* and in "Childhood of a Leader."

But the child raised under the influence of provincial complacency and tranquility underwent a metamorphosis. Admitted in 1925 to the Ecole Normale Supérieure, he became an intellectual during the period between World War I and World War II. In Paris he met Emanuel Mounier; in 1928 he received his degree in philosophy; after finally completing his military service (he had earlier had the benefit of deferment), he began teaching in a provincial lycée, the one in Le Havre which was to provide him ten years later with the setting for *Nausea.*

Thus Sartre's adult life began during the period marked by the end of World War I and the beginning of World War II, and his literary life began in 1938 with the publication of the work in which he summed up the period that was drawing to a close. Called to Paris, he became acquainted with

Paul Nizan, published a few magazine articles, and wrote novels which publishers rejected.

Not until the publication of *Nausea* in 1938, at 33, did he meet with critical success, and not until publication of *The Flies* and *No Exit*, at 38, did he become famous. Between 1925 and 1938, he had time to experience fully all the seethings, hopes, illusions, and disappointments of the period between the two world wars.

And that is why *Nausea* and *The Wall*, Sartre's pre-war works, as well as parts of *Roads to Freedom*, reflect the growing lassitude of the Gidean who wanted to remain free and disengaged, and who asked himself the question, "Why free?" It is the moment when the child of the twentieth century, cut loose from prejudices and customs and dreaming of total freedom, realizes that his freedom is meaningless if it remains ineffectual and empty; and leaving aside for the moment Sartre's philosophical systematization, in a purely literary sense Roquentin in *Nausea* is Gide's hero who has now aged and who by disengaging himself from moral standards and conventions, by casting off the "cloak of customs" and ready-made contacts, and by making use of clear judgment and critical insight, discovers that he lacks the stuff of life, that he does indeed possess a freedom which nothing can distort or constrain but which in turn finds nothing to which it can be applied.

That is the drama of the generation of Gide, the generation of young men who reached their twenties around 1920 when Gide, long ignored, achieved fame and became the prince of youth, when post-war euphoria was reflected in the daring and ridiculous adventures in which brazen youth was king. Gide's

14

Lafcadio, Cocteau's Thomas the Imposter, Radiguet's heroes were intoxicated adolescents who believe in nothing except their precious freedom and their whims. Freedom and lucidity were their watchwords, and it was among this generation that Sartre grew up. Twenty years later we find these two values transposed in his work, transformed from boundless youthful exhilaration into harsh and tragic necessity.

For the flowering of the twenties soon gave way to disillusion, economic crises, and the rise of fascism; hard-won freedom turned to bitterness, the emptiness of freedom without commitment was felt, and even more important, it was discovered that *liberation from prejudices did not eliminate the tragic element of life or man's responsibility*. In 1933 *Man's Fate*, written by a man who had matured rapidly as a result of his departure from Europe, marked the turning point: license was giving way to destiny.

Thus this generation was becoming aware of the insufficiency of the values discovered during its adolescence. Lucidity and disengagement were degenerating into stagnation; the contumelious, impudent, whimsical adolescent portrayed by Cocteau was becoming a mature, hypercritical, disabused man; he had discovered that whimsicality could not endure, that surrealism was but a straw fire, and he felt that the seething world of 1938-1939 was about to erupt in violence and put an end to individual freedom. He saw above him the dark clouds but refused to recognize that a threat existed, and as for himself, since he had set individual virtues above all else, he felt a certain emptiness; exhilaration was followed by a quarantine which saw the disappearance of the "sweetness of life" of 1920-1925; this man who sat dejected at a table in a cafe was none other than Antoine Roquentin, the hero of *Nausea*.

And in spite of his disordered life, Roquentin had the courage to take up the problem again and to proclaim unequivocally the emptiness of Gidean freedom for his generation.

A great part of Sartre's success doubtless comes from the fact that he portrays one of the most lucid generations of our century—one that is the most lucid, perhaps, because it had its beginning immediately after World War I, during a time of intense fermentation, and one that subsequently proved abortive. Sartre's adult life began during the early years of the period between World War I and World War II, and his first great book is the last great novel of this same period.

Sartre is thus the last writer of the period between the two wars. In silence, like any one of a number of his contemporaries, he lived through this period with its exhilaration, its dreams, its gratuitous art, its surrealism, its premonitions of a storm long averted, its eventual lassitude over its unused lucidity, and he made his appearance in literature in 1937 by writing *Nausea,* its last chapter.

His lucid and disabused character Roquentin, with his wasted youth and hapless adventure, marks the end of an era, but *Nausea* does not stop there. Beyond recording a failure, it raises a question and provides an answer: our freedom and lucidity are worthless until given a meaning. The book gives a meaning to the negative side of freedom and, after suggesting that Roquentin is typical of the men who were twenty years old in 1920, announces that Sartre's next work, a mature one, will concern those who were twenty in 1940; thus *while it marks an end to the period between the two wars, it also signals the opening of the post-war era that lies ahead.*

* * *

After 1940 a new element appears in Sartre's works. Before 1940 problems were limited to the individual; Roquentin was a typical individualist hardly concerned with the course of history. Against this, *Roads to Freedom* shows man linked in spite of himself to the collective body of men and to the totality of events. Thus freedom and responsibility take on new significance. It can even be said that *Roads to Freedom* deliberately and explicitly constitutes a pivotal work. In it the men of 1938 are judged in terms of the spirit of France at the time of the Liberation. Though he provides a remarkable summation of the period between the two world wars and even experiences some pleasure in evoking it, Sartre *nevertheless adopts views which attempt to transcend it and which therefore tend to bridge two eras.* Those who were born in 1925 and who spent their adolescence under the occupation were quick to turn away from the writers whom they considered outmoded and of whom the most typical was Gide:

> A young middle-class Parisian finds freedom in Algeria; such a story interests us if it is effectively written. But between 1940 and 1944 adolescents did not have to go so far or follow such a devious course to become even more free and to find another freedom. . . . We are strangers to this romantic crisis which is consummated *before* our eyes in monotony.[6]

17

Never was a leader more impatiently awaited than during 1944 and 1945. In 1938 *Nausea* had put an end to the skeptical individualism characteristic of the period between the two wars; Sartre, having come to feel during the "phony war," captivity, and the Resistance, that responsibility "among men" was a necessary sequel to the rank individualism of the past, had already determined to come to grips with the issue. He found himself uniquely prepared to play the role which, according to his statements, was imposed on him rather than solicited by him.

He was among the first to understand that the individualism of the thirties had died on the squalid bench in the Rendez-Vous des Cheminots where Roquentin experienced nausea, and had prepared himself to transcend it and create new perspectives; it is in this sense that he did offer himself, perhaps without wishing to do so, as a guide in 1944. Thus the paradoxical success of a quasi-esoteric work whose depth can be plumbed only with difficulty and whose superficial atmosphere may seem disgusting is nevertheless explained by the fact that while it never ceases to come to grips with human destiny, the central problem of the literature of the twentieth century, it has as its focal point the vortex shared by successive generations oblivious of one another, the void of 1939-1944. From each side Sartre advances to the edge of the void: Roquentin is the extreme example of empty individualism culminating in anguish; Mathieu Delarue succeeds him and sacrifices himself, rejecting disengagement at the very moment that witnesses the birth of Oreste, his counterpart, in *The Flies*.

Outside the philosophical meaning which is its

transposition and sublimation, such is the contemporary significance of Sartre's work; he invites us in 1944 to judge from the perspectives of the moment our thoughts in 1938. Only the future will tell whether his influence is limited to the transitional role which was responsible for his literary success in 1945. There is every reason to believe that the most intensely "lived" part of his work is precisely the "passage and parade" of literary history over which he presided between *Nausea* and *Roads to Freedom*.

* * *

For World War II marked the turning point in his life. It neatly coincided with his discovery of his own work and thought.

Before 1939 Sartre had already written a philosophical treatise, *Imagination* (1938). *Nausea* (1938) and *The Wall* (1939), besides bringing him critical recognition, had given him access to the *Nouvelle Revue Française*, in which he published numerous articles. But before World War II his fame had scarcely reached beyond the informed public. Those who read him in 1938 on the advice of a classmate today may fondly recall Roquentin, who seemed like a hard, blunt, but open friend, and may regret seeing him transformed into a sovereign pontiff and spiritual confessor.

In 1939 appeared *The Emotions, Outline of a Theory*, and in 1940 his *Psychology of the Imagination*. Sartre was still a philosopher capable of writing a book like *Nausea* but not of living in, for, and by means of Parisian literary life. A few years of silence followed as a result of the war and his captivity; in

1943, however, *The Flies* burst like a bombshell and transformed a professor of philosophy into a dramatist. France in 1943 was in a state of suspended animation and the human meaning of his work was overshadowed by the calculated boldness of its allusions. Its political satire was unfortunately mingled with equal parts of religious satire. But in spite of the confusion which was perhaps to be expected at that time, the salient aspect of the play was its tone of revolt. The publication of *Being and Nothingness*, a heavy treatise on philosophy, met with success disproportionate to the philosophical awareness of the public. The semipolitical boldness of a dramatist had caused an obscure philosopher to become a writer with a huge following.

With the Liberation Sartre became, perhaps unwillingly, the man of the hour. It is pointless to call attention to the surge of publicity that contributed to his success. For five years new talent had been repressed while his was undisputed. He was the guiding light. Did he give in to pressure? All that is certain is that since that time he has published no philosophical works. His decision to give up teaching was unanimously lamented by his students and even by those most opposed to the initial postulates of his theory.

In 1944, and before the Liberation, performances of *No Exit*, interrupted by sirens and given in a theatre with make-shift lighting, announced a work unconcerned with the actual situation but imbued with more dramatic intensity than *The Flies*, whose Greco-Giralducian vocabulary might leave room for doubt.

By the end of 1944 Sartre's name had become a byword, and the "discovery" of this great new writer is equaled only by that of Paul Valéry twenty-five years earlier. But Sartre would not be courted by the world-lings and, for better or for worse, preferred the company of carefree youths and journalism. The singularity of his case seems to indicate that in spite of what critics may have said, his conduct required courage. In 1945 *The Reprieve* and *The Age of Reason* made his fictional work overshadow his philosophical work, and the ambitious title of the series *The Roads to Freedom* seemed to announce a fictional work as forceful as *Nausea* and even broader in scope. The first two volumes of the series, solidly grounded on the past, fulfilled half of the promise implied by the title; only the last volume, still unpublished, will allow us to draw a conclusion.

The literary life in its multiple forms continued to beckon the author. His response to the public's demand was proof of his talent if not of his intellectual progression. He wrote reports about the United States, completed *The Victors* and *The Respectful Prostitute* (1946), and during the same year gave a lecture, *Existentialism Is Humanism,* designed to sate snobs and dilettantes concerned with "problems." The title, which made no sense, was enough to cause some of his auditors to swoon.

The screen and even radio also laid claim on the versatility of Sartre. In 1947 he completed an excellent scenario, *The Chips Are Down*, which was produced by Julien Duvivier. Another scenario, *In the Mesh,* was never produced and was published without much fanfare, in 1949; though he had sacrificed his philosophy in the hope of winning a wider public than the one that establishes literary reputations, Sartre failed to find such an audience.

Meanwhile the evolution of his thought had convinced Sartre that the writer's first concern is with politics. He founded the monthly journal *Les Temps Modernes*; in his journal, in a series called "What Is Literature?" he defined the function of the man of letters. The writer must renounce universal ideals in favor of specific goals:

> Abstract intentions should not exist in isolation and send out into the void appeals which have no direct influence on the human condition in general . . . but should be actualized in their purity; ideal goals should be transformed into *immediate, material goals.*[7]

The preceding statement shows clearly the radical change which Sartre had undergone in giving up the description of *the human condition* in general in favor of immediate, material goals.

Baudelaire in 1947 and *Kean* in 1954 were still indicative of Sartre's predilection for case analyses, and he has been concerned by and large since the foundation of *Les Temps Modernes* with political analysis and even with action, having once tried, with David Rousset and Gérard Rosenthal, to found the *Rassemblement Démocratique Révolutionnaire*. Plays like *Dirty Hands* (1948), *Lucifer and the Lord* (1951), and *Nekrassov* (1955) are dramatic vulgarizations of political themes.

NOTES

Chapter I

1. Georges Bernanos, *Sous le Soleil de Satan* (Plon, 1926), p. 98.

2. *L'Age de raison*, pp. 16-17.

3. Sartre sometimes calls him Pablo (*Le Sursis,* p. 85), sometimes Pedro (*ibid.*, p. 182).

4. *L'Age de raison*, pp. 48-49.

5. Francis Jeanson, *Le Problème moral et la pensée de J.-P. Sartre*, pp. 17-18.

6. Paul Vallanies, "Nés en 1925," *Les Temps Modernes,* LXII, pp. 2047-2049.

7. "Qu'est-ce que la littérature?" *Situations* II, p. 293.

II. FROM THE GRATUITOUSNESS
OF EXISTENCE TO
HUMAN RESPONSIBILITY

A. ALONG THE BOULEVARD NOIR

In 1938 there appeared under the name of Jean-Paul Sartre a book entitled *Nausea,* to which the publisher had added the qualification "novel." It was really more like a metaphysical diary, kept by an uprooted intellectual, Antoine Roquentin. On reaching the age of thirty-five, after an adventurous life that seems hardly credible, Roquentin settles down in Bouville (Le Havre) to continue his scholarly research on an eighteenth-century rake and intriguer, M. de Rollebon. The fact is that our intellectual is bored with the local restaurant, the boulevard, and the public library. We are not convinced by his pompous statement:

> I have crossed the seas, I have left towns behind
> me and I have sought out the sources of streams
> and the depths of forests, and always I have gone
> on toward other towns. I have had women, I
> have fought with men. . . .[1]

Such a past seems unlikely, and we are prone to look upon him as a sad recluse and future Professor Delarue who to remain free has refused to commit himself in any way.

His portrayal of boredom was so effective that some found it morbid. He focuses attention on the most sordid and wretched aspect of solitude:

> I am alone, most people have returned to their homes, they are reading the evening paper while listening to the radio. Sunday is drawing to a close and has left them with a taste of ashes; their thoughts are already turning toward Monday. But for me there is neither Monday nor Sunday. There is but a ragged sequence of days. . . .[2]

Around Roquentin, there is no one except a shadow and a caricature of himself, a ludicrous character whom he meets at the public library and dubs the Self-Taught Man. Disgustedly he observes like a repulsive insect the Self-Taught Man, whose function in the novel is to represent in the most grotesque and sordid way the intellectual illusions of men, just as the middle class citizens of Bouville epitomize their moral hypocrisy. He is just an ordinary clerical worker who is obsessed by a passion for knowledge and who makes a pretense of using his knowledge to solve life's problems. Having undertaken the task of self-instruction, he spends his days reading in the library; with surprise Roquentin sees successive volumes pass through his hands—*Turf and Peat-Moss* by Larbalétrier, *Hitopadesa or Useful Instruction* by Lastex, *The Caudebec Arrow* by Julie Lavergne; then Roquentin understands that the Self-Taught Man is reading everything in the public library in alphabetical order according to authors. Roquentin, bored like all lonely people, accepts the companionship of just anybody and converses at times with the Self-Taught Man, who sees in him an educated and much traveled personage.

This puppet epitomizes the impotence and ridiculousness of the culture toward which Roquentin remains skeptical:

> From time to time I raise my head a little and see his scrawny neck protruding from his huge stiff collar. He wears shabby clothes, but the whiteness of his linen is dazzling. . . . I contemplate him with admiration. . . . One day, seven years ago . . . he walked ceremoniously into this room. He must have glanced over the numberless books that line the walls and said, in much the same way as Rastignac, "For us—all of human knowledge." Then he must have gone over and taken the first book from the first shelf. . . . Now he has reached L. K after J, L after K. He switched from the study of coleoptera to the quantum theory, from a work on Tamerlane to a Catholic pamphlet against Darwinism. . . . And the day is nearing when he will close the last volume on the last shelf to the extreme left and say, "And now? " [3]

Roquentin's uneasiness in the face of the simpleminded man's pretentions is as convincing as his lassitude in the face of his efforts to explain his notion of humanism:

His eyes question me and I nod my approval, but I sense that he is somewhat disappointed, that he would like a greater show of enthusiasm. What can I do? Is it my fault if everything he says echoes an idea or a quotation he has borrowed? If I again call to mind as he speaks the humanists I have known? [4]

The Self-Taught Man is perhaps the best character created by Sartre, and this in all probability stems from the fact that in him he put much of himself, or at least the part of himself that he wanted to reject. The figure of the Self-Taught Man, an easy prey to captious notions and the fascination of the printed page, is essentially a foil to all intellectuals. Everything he believes is everything Sartre himself believed for a moment or a month during the course of his intellectual development. He is the intellectual without critical judgment, the man who believes in higher syntheses and is deceived by elementary dialectics. Against this, Roquentin represents pure critical judgment, and only a composite portrait of both figures will reveal the real protagonist in *Nausea.* Finally, the Self-Taught Man will see his universe collapse the day he is expelled from the library for having timidly touched the bare arm of a young boy.

Apart from the central character, there are only a few episodical figures which magnify the depressing squalor of provincial life as seen by an outsider: the obsequious proprietress in the Rendez-Vous des Cheminots, a waiter, and the bust of Impétraz, Bouville's most illustrious son. A state examiner during the nineteenth century, Impétraz had shown a fondness for erudite little books; he symbolizes everything that is conventional in the mediocre existence of the little town. The hypercritical Roquentin refuses to participate in such an existence, preferring to smoke the tobacco of boredom along the Boulevard Noir:

> In taverns behind me people are drinking and playing cards. Here, nothing but darkness. . . . Sometimes a big truck whizzes down the street with a thunderous noise.[5]

Nor does anything ever happen, except one day when Roquentin discovers that the life of his eighteenth-century libertine bores him as much as everything else. Once there appears someone called Annie, a woman who had previously met Roquentin and who has ceased to believe in perfect moments—moments of exaltation that justify life.

Dubious poetry about morbid boredom, uninspiring walks along a deserted boulevard, trivial announcements read to while away the hours, perfunctory smiles leading up to an exchange of greetings with the smart set after Mass on Sunday morning, recognition of the false importance that men attribute to themselves in daily life—everything focuses attention on the basic idea in the book, which is that under normal circumstances *nothing justifies existence*.

And that is exactly why Sartre chose as a character Antoine Roquentin, for he is an extreme case. Alone, lacking both responsibilities and good taste, he is charged with *becoming aware* of the complete lack of justification of his hand-to-mouth existence. Others have petty concerns and petty joys, like the man who goes into a pastry shop holding a little boy by the hand and comes out with a pretty package tied with a blue or pink ribbon; or they may be parties to hypocrisy on a vast scale—as shipping or industrial magnates, mayors or judges who pretend to devote themselves to the public good and thereby amass fortunes. But in the eyes of this isolated observer, their lives are the lives of puppets and Roquentin can but echo Pascal in contrasting with diversions and mundane pleasures the necessity of *justifying* his life. Nor is Roquentin less severe than Pascal, for even though he has ceased to believe in all the illusions and all the impostures through which the people of Bouville hide from themselves their destiny, he still finds his life empty and disoriented.

His attitude is what gives the book its dark tone. And even though his attitude epitomizes a reduction to absurdity, we must not forget that he is no more pessimistic than Pascal. Day-to-day life, whether based on imposture or critical judgment, is unjustified.

Roquentin senses this in himself as well as in others, and he is then overcome by Nausea.

* * *

For in this plotless novel, Nausea provides the key incident. We all sense it when suddenly during a moment of lassitude we have the impression that we are wasting our time, that life must be something more than this. Nausea, to the extent that it represents our awareness of the fact that our acts are not automatically justified, is found also in the works of Christian writers.

For often all our actions amount to nothing more

than vain agitation and are of spurious importance. And still *we are there, responsible,* and if our life is vain or even insufficiently justified, we then feel that our existence is intolerable and are gripped by a ghastly fear. Who has not felt this shock and this anguish, perhaps on waking suddenly in the early hours of morning and finding it difficult to accept his usual behavior and his accustomed goals in life? Sartre's Nausea is not an exceptional state but the expansion of a feeling experienced and promptly rejected by every normal man, and one studied by doctors. It is at once the question "But why am I living?" and the terrifying vertigo that results from not *sensing* an immediate reply. To be sure, once we regain our composure, we find answers and adduce reasons. Sartre cleared the ground by anticipating all our answers and reasons and putting them in the mouth of the Self-Taught Man. Thus, although a Christian may not always follow Sartre, it is worth noting that his starting point, Nausea, is the same as that of Christian reflection; on examining his everyday life, his vulgar life based on illusions, deceptions, and conventions, man feels himself *profoundly unjustified and gripped by terror.* On seeing that his existence has not acquired a meaning of its own, he is afraid and would like *not to be there;* but his responsibility pursues and overpowers him, and that is why he forces himself to forget as quickly as possible his moment of Nausea. But he *is there,* he feels that his existence is unjustified, and *he is of necessity afraid.* At the crux of Sartre's philosophy is the notion of "being-there-in-the-world," and it is the notion of the anguish of existing that makes it possible to compare Sartre with men as different from him as Pascal or Kierkegaard.

B. THE ANGUISH OF EXISTING

Thus exceptional circumstances of solitude and disgust make of Roquentin a man in whom the anguish of existing, instead of manifesting itself as sporadic flashes that quickly disappear, becomes an enduring reality. Like other existential philosophers Sartre sees even in this fundamental anguish human reality in its entirety, the very reality whose study and elucidation will result in the philosophical conclusion that "We are anguish." [6] Roquentin is then for Sartre the subject of an experiment, a case for clinical observation. He *lives* the feeling that Sartre wishes to study and records in his diary:

> Monday, January 29, 1932. Something has happened to me, there can no longer be any doubt about it. It came like a sickness, not abruptly or insistently but slowly and insidiously; I felt a little uneasy, that's all. Once there, it refused to go away; it stayed quietly and I was able to persuade myself that nothing was wrong, that it was a false alarm. Now it is spreading.[7]

This book is an analysis by the subject himself of an obsession which is inherent in man but which man ordinarily tries to mask through vain agitation. Roquentin even goes so far as to insist on setting down an exact description of his case:

> My purpose is not to write for the sake of writing. *I write in order to clarify certain circumstances.* I have no use for literature. Everything must be set down as it comes to mind, without groping for words.[8]

Roquentin is actually in the state of *detachment* required by all reflection on the essence of things and by all striving, even in a religious sense; he no longer clings to anything, and the abandonment of his last project, his scholarly study of M. de Rollebon's life, symbolizes his detachment. He enters what the mystics call spiritual oblivion:

> But I can explain what I see to no one. All I know is that I slip ever so gently to the bottom of the water, toward fear.[9]

Every thought is astounding, and Roquentin is first astounded by his existence in the world and by the existence of things. These things, once he has broken away from routine patterns of human observation, appear to him naked, divorced from the meaning that we habitually attribute to them as tools; they appear to be petrified objects in a nightmarish world, as pure and alien as in the works of the surrealists: "The Boulevard Noir is inhuman. Like a mineral. Like a triangle."[10] Only a pitiable outcast and his monotonous strolls through a deserted town could evoke the inhuman aspect that things acquire when we reflect on them. That they exist and force themselves on us then becomes scandalous; we no longer know how to justify their existence. Awareness of our own existence causes Nausea; awareness of the existence of things causes terror.

> Now I see; I recall more distinctly what I felt the other day by the seashore while holding a pebble. It was a sweetish sort of disgust. And how unpleasant it was! And it came from the

pebble, I'm sure it oozed out of the pebble in my hands.[11]

His fear becomes even a sort of sickly hallucination and withdrawal in the face of a world with no pre-determined meaning:

> Objects ought not to touch you, for they aren't alive. You use them, you put them back in place, you live among them; they are useful, that's all there is to it. But they touch me, and I can't stand it. I'm afraid to come in contact with them. It's as if they were living creatures.[12]

Then he becomes aware of *contingency*, that is, the *gratuitousness* of himself and everything around him. The trees along the boulevard are there, and the root of the chestnut-tree, but they might just as well not be there, they might be different; he is there, but is there any profound reason for that?

> The essential thing is contingency. I mean that by definition existence is not necessity. To exist is *to be there,* simply; existents appear, they let you bump into them, but you can never deduce them. . . . *Everything—this garden, this town—is gratuitous; I myself am gratuitous.* When the truth finally dawns on you, you feel disgusted and your head begins to swim, like the other evening; that's Nausea.[13]

Nausea would indeed be a purely morbid feeling if one cultivated the awareness of gratuitousness and lapsed into a total, hopeless nihilism like that caricatured by Alphonse Daudet in *Tartarin dans les Alpes.* But such nihilism is impossible, for it entails self-destruction; at the crux of the vertigo accompanying Nausea is not so much the verification of the gratuitousness of the world and ourselves as the discovery that *in spite of this gratuitousness our existence lacks justification. The sequel of Nausea is the responsibility to ourselves that we are forced to recognize by virtue of the simple fact that we exist.*

This responsibility, which will later assume a moral significance, is evidently felt at the outset as horror since, at the first sign of it, we would like to reject it. But we can not evade the issue, for *we do exist* and we are afraid of the self that exists and must seek its justification:

> My thought is me; that is why I can stop. I exist because I think . . . and I can not keep myself from thinking. At this very moment—I exist *only because I'm horrified by existing;* I pull *myself* up out of the nothingness toward which I aspire; hatred and disgust over existing are simple means of *making myself exist,* of plunging into existence. Thoughts surge up in my wake, like vertigo; I feel them surging up behind my head . . . if I give in, they will come up in front, between my eyes; and I always give in, and the thought swells, swells boundlessly until it fills me completely and renews my existence.[14]

The apparently monotonous pages of Antoine Roquentin's diary express the vertiginous derangement of a man who has been divested of all the false significations that we attribute to objects and to ourselves and who becomes aware of the terrible element which man, unjustified and surrounded *by unjustifiable things,* has at the crux of his situation:

> I place my hand on the bench but hurriedly withdraw it— it *exists.* This thing on which I am seated and on which I place my hand is called a bench . . . I murmur, "It's a bench," somewhat in the manner of an exorcism. But the word sticks to my lips and refuses to take its place on the thing.[15]

Like the surrealists, Roquentin has withdrawn from all the things around him their ordinary meaning and is probing their profound reality, which is revealed as absurd but insistent and importunate:

> Things are divorced from their names. They are there—grotesque, obstinate, enormous—and it seems idiotic to call them benches or to hazard a remark about them. I am surrounded by Things, by nameless things. Alone, nameless, defenseless, they surround me; they are under me, behind me, above me. They require nothing, they are not obtrusive; they simply exist.[16]

The same vertigo takes hold of him at the sight of the root of a chestnut-tree:

> Just now I was in the park. The root of the chestnut-tree plunged into the earth right beneath my bench. I no longer remembered that it was a root. Words had vanished and with *them the signification of things, the uses to which they*

35

are put, the faint bench marks which men have drawn on their surfaces. . . . And then I had this sudden revelation. It was breath-taking. Until a few days ago I had never realized the meaning of "exist." Ordinarily existence remains hidden. It is there, all around me; I am existence; it is impossible to say two words without speaking of it; and last but not least, it can't be touched.[17]

This example explains better than anything else the original meaning of the word existentialism. The opposite philosophical attitude, essentialism, holds that whatever exists contains in itself its meaning along with its existence; against this, existentialism holds that *whatever exists manifests its existence* but is initially unjustified. That is how facticity—the irremediable contingency of our "being-there," of our "purposeless and groundless existence" [18]—makes its appearance. Still, we ought not to confuse this starting point with absolute pessimism, for among the groundless existents there may be one, like man, with the specific function of acquiring a meaning and a justification. But this notion will not be developed until later. In the semi-hallucinatory state which makes existence appear naked and in the raw, which reveals to him a world devoid of excuses and alibis, Roquentin sees the dissolution of the signification that he has been attributing to the most familiar object, to his face which is reduced to a hideous presence on which he is no longer able to superimpose an interpretation:

I shudder; I get up. In the wall is a white hole, the mirror. It is a trap. I know I'm going to

fall into the trap. There it is. The grey thing
has just appeared to me in the mirror. I move
closer to it and look at it; I can't break away.[19]

And even his hand becomes alien and absurd as
soon as it is considered, not as an effective and therefore meaningful instrument, but as an object; he
examines it as if he were a debilitated patient:

> I see my hand resting on the table. It is alive,
> it is me. It opens up, the fingers unfold and
> point. It is on its back. . . . It looks like an ani-
> mal turned on its back. . . . I feel my hand. It
> is me; I am these two writhing animals at-
> tached to my arms.[20]

Strangely enough, the "alien hand" is a recurrent
theme in Rilke, who relates that as a child he had
stooped over to pick up a pencil under the table:

> I could distinguish the wall from the base
> trimmed by a light plinth; I took my bearings
> from the legs of the table; and suddenly I rec-
> ognized my own extended hand; its fingers
> spread out, it was moving independently, feel-
> ing its way along the base, almost like an
> aquatic animal. I recall watching its action
> almost with curiosity; it seemed to me to know
> things which I had never taught it, to see
> it groping down there, employing movements
> that I had never observed.[21]

And under circumstances closer to Roquentin's,
that is, at a moment when things appear in their

intolerable crudeness, divested of the sheen usually spread over them by commonplace patterns of behavior, Perken in Malraux's *The Royal Way* experiences in dying the same sense of astonishment at the sight of his hand:

> For several days he had been looking at it repeatedly in this way: free, apart from him. There, at rest on his thigh, it was looking at him. . . . This hand was there, white, fascinating. . . . Not enormous but simple, natural, yet as vivacious as an eye.[22]

C. REFUSAL OF ALIBIS

There are, however, many means of saving life from the terrifying lack of predetermined signification that men prefer to ignore as a result of their fear of finding themselves obliged to create one. Roquentin had once been the friend of a woman who thought that if life is a loose tissue of insignificant moments there are at least moments when it *takes a certain shape* and acquires a meaning:

> She always wanted to realize "perfect moments." If the moment failed to lend itself to this, she lost interest in everything, and life vanished from her eyes; she dragged herself along indolently, like an overgrown girl passing through the awkward age.[23]

And Annie had forced Roquentin to adopt certain attitudes, to avoid certain clumsy patterns of be-

havior and certain dissonances in order that existence might at times yield through these precaution-
ary measures perfect moments, a sort of echo of
eternity. But Annie reappears in *Nausea* only to
say that "perfect moments do not exist." Through
her Sartre seeks to rebuff and to reject the temptation of estheticism—Gide's gratuitous acts and Mallarmé's and Valéry's pure objects.

Proust had dedicated himself to the task of *recon-
structing the past*. From an experience lived in the
present and perhaps loosely connected and shapeless, the magic of memory, of vanished time, and of
art can yield a creation which contains its own justification. And Roquentin seeks again to banish this
illusion and this vain consolation:

> I wanted the moments of my life to follow in
> an orderly fashion like those of a remembered
> life. I might as well have tried to catch time
> by the tail.[24]

Art which in the retelling lends to a series of shapeless events an appearance of coherence is a lie
through which man masks reality:

> To recount the present in the past is to resort
> to an artifice, to create a strange and beautiful
> world, as rigid as a Mardi Gras mask that be-
> comes an object of terror when a real, *living
> man* puts it over his face.[25]

To avoid the pitfall opened by the magic through
which the artist transfigures life and as a result
avoids raising the questions that must be raised con-

39

cerning it, Sartre wrote none of his novels in the past; *Nausea* as well as *Roads to Freedom* and most of the short stories in *The Wall* were written in the present.

* * *

But do not most men attribute a meaning to their existence without having to pass through nausea? Does not the ordinary man believe in what he is doing?

Such naive, unpremeditated belief and confidence are the very things that provoke Sartre's ridicule. In their pretended earnestness men like Roquentin fail to raise penetrating questions and pretend to justify the crux of their existence through their prejudices, their patterns of behavior, and their superficial conventions.

With *Nausea* Sartre introduces those whom he calls *salauds*. These are people ordinarily designated by the less expressive term Pharisees. They lead a quiet, confident life and *believe themselves justified*, in contrast to Roquentin, who by living his anguish seeks to pose more urgently the question of justification. They readily believe that their lives are coherent and therefore grow fat and unyielding in the attitude of complacency that Anouilh calls happiness:

> Race of Abel, race of the just, race of the rich, how calmly you speak. It's nice, isn't it, to have for yourselves both God and the State. It's nice to think sometimes like your father and your father's father. . . .[26]

Sartre, like Pascal and like many of his contemporaries, denounces in no uncertain terms the false sense of security of men who try to become important enough to believe in themselves, in their superficial lives, and thereby to elude the fundamental problems of existence. Their serious air strikes Roquentin as he enters a restaurant:

> I look around the room. What a farce! All the people are sitting there, looking serious and eating. No, they are not eating; they are fortifying themselves for the task that lies ahead. Each of them has his own little personal bias which prevents him from being aware of his existence; every single one of them believes himself indispensable to someone or to something.[27]

The mock importance through which the *salauds* fashion a pleasant, reassuring image of themselves and hide from themselves the most acute and agonizing facet of their freedom and their responsibility is tied to their reputation, their social position, their unshakable confidence in their rights. "But is that enough to justify a man?" asks Roquentin when at the museum he views in succession the portraits of the middle-class citizens of Bouville, irritating in their inviolable respectability and in their haughtiness:

> Not one of those portrayed had died childless or intestate, not one had died without the last sacraments. That day, as on other days, with everything in order with respect to both God and the world, they slipped gently into death, to go and lay claim to that part of eternal life to which they were entitled. For they were en-

41

titled to everything—to life, to work, to wealth, to authority, to respect, and at the end to immortality.[28]

Roquentin takes leave of the museum with a diatribe directed against the varnished portraits of men who, distracted by the feeling of their importance and by civic honors, have never been uneasy about the meaning of their lives:

> Farewell, fair roses set in your little painted sanctuaries.
> Farewell, fair roses, our pride and reason for being.
> Farewell, *Salauds*.[29]

That external and worldly importance is not enough to constitute a true moral life and true human sincerity, and that overconfidence based on respectability is a worthless illusion, is not a new theme but one already exploited by Bossuet as well as by Pascal. In an age which like ours has broken down the values of society, however, it acquires increased importance and appears in all our great writers, in Gide as well as in Malraux, in Pirandello as well as in Anouilh. Strangely enough, Sartre's brutality and the crudeness of his diatribe bring to mind Léon Bloy, and his farewell to the *salauds* suggests *Cochons-sur-Marne* and *Mémoires d'un entrepreneur de démolitions*.

Sartre rebels against "values" to the extent that they are congealed products of a civilization and are susceptible of being transformed from lived realities into alibis for hypocrisy. And Sartre is critical of moral values degraded by the fatal stamp of conventionality since they can become a mask instead of a source of uneasiness, a mock justification instead of a responsibility. This is what Péguy meant in speaking of a vast mystical element which degenerates into a political element. Sartre shows an unmistakable tendency to stress the absolute sincerity, lucidity, and responsibility of the individual to the detriment of collective values and "morality" which changes all too often into a disguise for insincerity. The attitude which Sartre systematizes had been vigorously defended by Gide and generally sanctioned by our age; it is the attitude that led Bernanos to attack "moral beasts."

We have dealt at length with Sartre's first book because it contains the essence of his thought: a reduction to absurdity and a purification which nullify all the excuses that cowardly men invent in order to avoid raising questions and experiencing in its fullness and in the absence of alibis the total gratuitousness of the world and the self, and as a consequence, the unveiling of the freedom and responsibility which compel man to create the justifications which he does not find predetermined in existence.

D. AN ACCOUNT OF NAUSEA

Nausea is not an aberrant phenomenon. Sartre, perhaps because the style of his book is too forceful, confers on the anguish of existing an awesome and even a sordid power and may by so doing offend

43

sensitive readers; even so, he is simply emphasizing and making more oppressive a theme that is easily identifiable in the works of his contemporaries. The feeling that life is unjustified is as easily detected in Camus' Stranger as in Julien Green's Emmanuel Fruges, the Self-Taught Man in a different guise:

> "Why was I created?" he asks ". . . I have grown old before my time and am as wretched and black as a rat. . . . Was it for the glory of God?"[30]

Also unjustified in the face of eternity are the heroes of Malraux.

It would seem that here we have in the place of intense feeling a statement of the general position of the twentieth-century writer, who studies man, not in the context of conventions and ready-made doctrines which might help him to live, but stripped naked and brought face to face with his stark destiny and with the human condition. As early as 1911, the Christian writer Miguel de Unamuno was already describing nausea and making it the basis of every system of thought, even the most methodical: "The personal and effective starting point of any philosophy or religion is the tragic sense of life." [31]

Sartre is here describing twentieth-century man, who has broken further and further away from external laws and assumed to an ever increasing degree a strictly personal responsibility for his life. Since Nietzsche it has often been said that "God is dead." Between the nineteenth century and ours, it is not so much God that is dead as a whole set of values halfway between God and man, a set of myths and demigods which philosophers call values. We can be sure that even if new values appear in our age, the system of values that prevailed during the past century has been torn asunder. Goodness, Beauty, Truth, and Justice, conventional notions bandied about by philosophers, were jeopardized by the inexorable evolution of morals and of circumstances, by a new psychology, by the modification of scientific criteria for investigation and verification, and by the obsolescence of established values which society by dint of usage has reduced to the state that normally results from half-hearted and hypocritical utilization—debasement. Every time Beauty is invoked to justify academism, the concept of beauty suffers; every time an unjust act is condoned, justice dies; every time truth is called an irrational and partisan conviction, in the eyes of men the light of truth is extinguished. The rapid, cataclysmic events that have characterized the period extending from 1870 to the present have entailed a frightening destruction of myths and concepts, and that is why such men as Unamuno, Péguy, Pirandello, Gide, and Huxley, and in an even more striking manner Julien Green, Malraux, Camus, Graham Greene, and the German expressionists, have adopted and advocated since the beginning of the century a perceptive attitude which no longer attributes to man a set of notions and conventions to serve as guides, since they quickly fall into disuse and encourage laxity, stereotyped behavior, and hypocrisy in a society in which they are unstable and which depreciates them through frantic and at times vile usage; their attitude reveals man rather as a lost child who has nothing to guide him or to help him, and this is indeed the situation that lends to the works just cited an atmosphere of anxiety and tragedy.

Nausea is but the transposition on a reduced scale, in the form of a lived emotion, of the prevalent esthetic and ethical values of society. Writers like Graham Greene and Albert Camus depict heroes who support no enduring values, who depend on no one for guidance, and who must build their destiny without outside help; similarly Roquentin has the feeling that life by itself is unjustified. In 1908 G. K. Chesterton, though he had just been converted to Catholicism, described in *A Man Named Thursday* a hero who, enlisting in the forces of Good, later served as a spy for the forces of Evil and discovered that their leader was the same. Chesterton was the forerunner of Georges Bernanos, for whom even a saint like Father Donissan in *Sous le Soleil de Satan* is not sure whether God or Satan has hold of him, so intimately linked within him are the two powers. The central character in Graham Greene's *The Ministry of Fear* is also a man without *recourse,* sincere but equally suspect to the spies against whom he struggles and to the police who pursue them; in the same way Andrews in *The Man Within* is sought by both smugglers and customs officers.

Thus values and, in the interest of simplification, Good and Evil are felt in our century (and, in the preceding examples, by three Catholic writers) to be commingled and so skillfully blended that man must live alone and helpless in his confusion and yet must still affirm his responsibility. Nothing tells us in this inextricable melee that our acts are justified, yet we owe it to ourselves to justify them.

Roquentin, on a plane which is just as valid

though less tragic, less edifying, and more sordid, feels that everything is gratuitous and that by the very fact of existing he must go beyond this gratuitousness. In the face of his responsibility he is afraid, just as the heroes of Chesterton, Bernanos and Graham Greene are afraid. But his fear and his nakedness at least point up irrefutably the responsibility which they predicate and which Sartre calls freedom.

E. CONSCIOUSNESS OF THINGS

Metaphysics is concerned with prescriptions for *justifying* the world and man. But Sartre rejects the metaphysical, that is, the unverifiable; he refuses to *imagine* behind consciousness a supporting mind, or behind Things a separate existence.

He therefore gives a simple description of the life of consciousness, the only reality that man *experiences*. And the distinguishing trait of consciousness is never to be itself but always to be attentiveness to an external object. "All consciousness is consciousness of something," [32] he wrote in 1940. Taking up Husserl's formula, he later wrote:

> My consciousness never exists in the abstract but only because it thinks of a tree or of Pierre's face; it manifests itself only by imagining something other than itself; it is born of something which it is not. [33]

It exists only to the extent that it is tied to external objects, and it needs them in order to exist.

These objects are Things. They need nothing in

order to exist, for they are there, massive, shapeless, as they appear in *Nausea*. They obtrude, and when I have a sheet of paper before me, I can not make it be anything other than what it is. I can not make it not be white:

> One thing is certain, and that is that the white sheet that I observe can not be the product of my spontaneity. The inert form, which is beyond all conscious spontaneities and which must be observed and gradually learned, is what is called a *thing*.[34]

What is the relation between Things which are there, as impudent as a challenge, and consciousness, which exists only by caressing them and conceiving of them? Here Sartre builds an ontology, a philosophical description of the world. These Things he calls being. They exist in themselves (they constitute the in-itself) but they are in no way exact.

It is consciousness that illuminates them, that delineates form within the chaotic world of Things and gives it meaning; it is consciousness that makes of a meaningless agglomeration an outline, a chair, a definite object. Thus when consciousness says "there is a chair," it is separating from the chaotic world of Things a tiny portion of matter and conferring on it a structure and a meaning. It becomes indifferent to the rest of the world in order to consider the chair; to delineate the chair within a maze of phenomena, it assumes that everything else does not exist; it relegates everything else into Nothingness.

> This assumes a delimitation of being within being. . . . The being considered is *this* and out-

side of this, nothing. The artilleryman who is shown a target is careful to aim his cannon in a certain direction to the exclusion of every other direction.[35]

To perceive is then to *detach* an object from all other phenomena. It is also to become aware of this object, that is, to think of it while separating oneself from it. When consciousness sees a chair, it performs two operations: it forms the idea of chair, saying "There is a chair" and yet at the same time posits itself as apart from the chair, adding "But I am not the chair."[36]

Consciousness is nothing by itself except the power to delimit the world, that is, to deny one part and also to deny that it is identifying itself with that part through "a withdrawal effected with respect to Things." It is the power to "set itself outside of Being,"[37] and Sartre, designating it as for-itself, calls it "a being through which nothingness comes into things."[38]

* * *

The assimilation of consciousness and Nothingness might at first seem pessimistic and diabolical. But it really hinges on nothing more than the conventions and peculiarities of philosophical terminology. Like many other philosophers, Sartre contrasts consciousness with Things and gives to things the name Being; it is obvious that consciousness should start from the side of Nothingness, which is the contrasting term. This nothingness justifies no metaphysical shudder, for consciousness "nihilates" only in that it has the power to choose. To give a meaning

49

to a thing, it needs to separate it from other things by pushing them back into nothingness. *Nihilation is but the power to articulate and confer meaning on reality.* If consciousness were only Being, it would be petrifaction and not freedom; the result is that in Sartre's theory the term nothingness does not degrade but rather ennobles consciousness.

Sartre must not be looked upon as a necromancer and a spirit of negation simply because in his philosophical treatises he practices nihilation. In a general sense, and according to an inaccurate but useful oversimplification, to nihilate is to think—that is, to choose, to eliminate, to interpret. Thus with all his sophisticated terms, Sartre is merely stating that *man is consciousness that wrenches itself away from things and gives them a meaning.* There we have a clear, straightforward, appropriate, commonplace thought, and one that can hardly be judged reprehensible. Sartre may be wrong in designating as nihilation the withdrawal of consciousness from objects, but he does not make any apocalyptical affirmation. Though the word Nothingness generally has an unpleasant connotation, for Sartre it signifies the emergence of consciousness above things, the detachment of consciousness from matter. Man is "negativity" to the extent that even a slight perception prompts him to say to himself "I see a stone, and I am not this stone." It is in this sense that Sartre is an antimaterialist.

Sartre tried to reconcile philosophical realism and idealism. The existence of matter provides a basis for realism and constitutes its initial postulate; it fails, however, to explain how matter could have formed a reality as distinct from itself as the mind identified through subjective intuition. Against this, idealism has as its first postulate consciousness; it fails, however, to explain how consciousness can know objects in the external world.

To resolve the difficulty Sartre *reinforced the link between consciousness and Things* by making them interdependent; without consciousness Things are but they are nothing other than a meaningless chaos. Without Things, consciousness does not even exist, for its life consists of imagining them. Since everything is based on the relation between consciousness and Things, Sartre holds that as a consequence of his initial postulate, survival and the existence of God are inconceivable. But in another sense Sartre is again an antimaterialist, for even though he makes the existence of consciousness subject to the existence of Things, he refuses to grant that matter gives birth to thought.

It follows that he is not a proponent of materialistic and positivistic atheism in the traditional sense. For as a philosopher he even scorns science and, using consciousness as his starting point, uses matter only as an antagonistic force which, though necessary for consciousness, loses its importance by virtue of the fact that it has no meaning unless one is conferred on it by consciousness. He therefore discredits scientific discoveries, and for him the revelation of the structure of the atom is but another manifestation of imagination in men confronted by things: "Doubtless Taine's heavy stones have been replaced by sprightly protean mists, but these mists have not ceased to be things." [39] He feels that at bottom theories of the atom are unimportant, that no matter what its appearance, the material universe is the creature of consciousness.

Reality is in his view a product of human consciousness. His position is justifiable, for it is true that consciousness is responsible for whatever we know or imagine. But his initial postulate inevitably dominates and characterizes his whole philosophy. The starting point is always responsible for the incompatibility of philosophical doctrines. Sartre's is one of the simplest. An example of one more vast in scope and therefore most refractory is that of Spinoza who postulates an infinite substance and then studies its modifications and attributes. "First let us conceive of the general idea of everything that is or can be," says Spinoza. "Then let us examine the diverse modifications which the Whole undergoes." "Since all reality is accessible to us only through consciousness," says Sartre, "let us study only consciousness." The only difference between the two is attributable to their original positions, and neither is foolish. Such is Sartre's initial postulate. It is open to but one criticism: the unlimited possibility of choosing others.

F. FREEDOM CONDEMNED TO GIVE A MEANING TO THE WORLD

Human consciousness exists only as a free reflection that plays on the surface of petrified things and gives them a meaning. Its very mode of existence implies a constant effort on the part of man. If defined as the possibility of giving a signification to things, it is sheer activity. This activity, this necessity of choosing at every instant a perspective for viewing the world constitutes freedom. Paradoxically, our freedom imposes on itself a limitation, for we are free to confer the meaning of our choice on anything we choose, but at the same time we are obliged to confer meanings on things, to imagine, to interpret, and to choose.

Our freedom, which is our consciousness, entails necessity since it exists only insofar as it imagines something; exists only as a function of an external object. "To know is to burst out . . . to flow outward, beyond oneself, toward something else."[40] To the extent that man is being detached from things, he is not being but freedom. He is aware of "the imperceptible distance which things reveal"[41] to him and which forever separates him from them. In a sense, man dominates the existence of things since he sets himself apart from them in order to know them, but then he feels that his close association with the world is shattered, that he is an exile, and he sluggishly regrets not being one of the things that need make no effort to exist, for his own existence entails the constant employment of his freedom:

> He stretched out his hands and ran them slowly over the stone in the balustrade. It was rugose, cracked, a petrified sponge still warm from the afternoon sun. It was there, enormous and massive, enclosing in itself the shattered silence and compressed darkness which are the inside of things. It was there: a plenitude. He would have liked to cling to the stone, melt into it, glut himself on its opaqueness, on its composure. But it could afford him no relief; it was outside him forever.[42]

Consciousness is barren and empty if we lack the courage to make it live, to commit it to a project:

> Consciousness forgotten, abandoned between these walls, under the grey sky. And this is the meaning of its existence: it is conscious of being superfluous. It attenuates, spreads out, tries to lose itself on the brown wall, in the length of the street lamp, or out there in the evening dusk.[43]

But in this very despair appears a value: freedom. It is precisely because "consciousness is not what it is" that it is free; its awesome grandeur springs from its exile. If it were like objects, it would be immobile existence, smug and settled; it would lack the frightening and marvelous power of freedom revealed in the bitterness of an irresolute existence.

> "Outside. Everything is outside: the trees on the wharf, the two houses on the bridge that take on a pink hue at night, above my head the frozen leap of Henry IV. Everything that is heavy. Inside nothing, not even a phantom; there is no *inside*, nothing. Me: nothing. I am free," he said, his mouth dry.[44]

Because man *is* nothing, *he has to be, to make himself*:

> I am nothing, I have nothing. As inseparable from the world as light and yet exiled, like light, sliding along the surface of stones and

of the water, and nothing ever grapples me or causes me to run aground. Outside. Outside. Outside the world, outside the past, outside myself. Freedom is exile, and I am condemned to be free.[45]

Such is the dramatic position of consciousness in the world.

It first apprehends itself as absolutely gratuitous, groundless and purposeless, uncreated, unjustifiable, having no claim to existence other than the sole fact that it already exists. It could not find outside itself pretexts, excuses, or reasons for being; things cannot exist without its first being conscious of them; things have no meaning other than that which it sees fit to attach to them.[46]

For if man does not choose, if he does not accept his role which is always to imagine and to illuminate an external object, then like Roquentin, he endures indefinitely the anguish of existing. His existence remains unjustified so long as it is not summed up in the form of an interpretation of the world to which it will thereafter be committed. But if it then appears gratuitous to itself, it can not tolerate its gratuitousness, for it is still *there*. The sole function of consciousness is to confer a meaning on whatever surrounds it; when consciousness fails to carry out its natural function, it then becomes importunate. The result is that man would like to efface himself, to lift from the world the thought which is he and which tortures him by virtue of its uselessness:

Goetz (abruptly): Take this thought from me! Take it away! *Make me forget myself!* Change me into an insect.[47]

And in *Dirty Hands* Hugo suffers the same torture:

"There are many thoughts in my head. I must get rid of them . . . *What am I doing here?* Is it right for me to want what I want?" [48]

For consciousness alone is charged with giving a meaning to the world. Powerless to elude its inherent power, it is terrified:

Once a man has found himself through the cogito there can be no question of his getting lost again. The pit and darkness disappear; man is everywhere the measure of all things; wherever he is he sheds light, he sees only what he illuminates, and he determines the signification of all things.[49]

Human life, which impregnates things with meaning, is by nature perpetual striving, and if men tire of their ceaseless activity, if they falter in their struggle to achieve lucidity and to make decisions, things no longer have a meaning and their existence seems "dull, obscene, gratuitous." [50] They feel that they are superfluous:

"I want to leave, to go somewhere where I would really be *in my place* and fit in. . . . But my place is nowhere; I don't belong." [51]

Afraid that he has not sufficiently justified his life, Henri also feels that he is superfluous:

"No, I don't belong anywhere. No one will ever miss me. The subways are crowded, and the restaurants are chock-full; every place bristles with heads gorging on trifles. I slipped out of the world and it was still full. Like an egg. The fact is that I was not indispensable.[52]

And Jupiter in *The Flies* shows Oreste that man is not an object with a place in the world but a consciousness exiled to the world:

"You don't belong here, intruder. You are in the world like a splinter in the flesh, like a poacher in a seigniorial forest. . . ."[53]

Yet this intruder, this exile, is the only being through whom meanings appear in the world.

And that is how consciousness finds its true "self." It conquers the world that sentenced it to exile through its projects, through the meanings it confers and the transformations it imposes on that world.

* * *

A simple description of consciousness implies a moral philosophy if it shows the immobility and imbecility of things as well as their gratuitousness and that of consciousness, and if it also shows how consciousness is empowered and constrained to illuminate things. To imagine the world as required by our conscious life is to interpret it and to "commit" to it through our interpretation our future action.

Of course man would prefer to have only to "live out his life," to receive an existence which would

57

not need to be justified, simply to exist like a thing, free from responsibility. But such is not his lot.

> Perhaps we *are not* for ourselves like things. Perhaps we simply *are not* at all. Always in question, always being postponed, perhaps we must perpetually *make* ourselves.[54]

Is that not automatically the basic characteristic of man since his consciousness boils down to nothing more than freedom and signification? No, for the freedom which is "given" and merely given to us must be made efficient through an effort of our part, as Mathieu realizes in *Roads to Freedom*:

> But what is the purpose of freedom if not to make possible commitment? You spent thirty-five years in getting clean, and the result is emptiness.[55]

Here we see again the drama which the cult of an irresponsible lucidity entailed in some measure for the post-war generation; and this particular coincidence reveals Sartre's personal philosophy as a transposition of the history of literature and morals.

Consciousness is the palpitation of things by a power other than itself—man—and an indefinite freedom to name them and confer on them meaning; and this freedom, though inalienable and given by nature, must be shaped if it is to manifest itself and acquire value. Man to whom this power was given is guilty if he does not put it to use, and if he is afraid of it he feels empty and dull:

He was alone on the bridge, alone in the world, and no one could set him straight. "I am free *for nothing*," he thought wearily. . . . Mathieu reached out to the surface of things and they did not feel him.[56]

Having withdrawn from man everything that could reassure him, Sartre entrusts to him a terrible gift, his freedom through which he can again find everything that he has lost. And he must use his freedom fully in order to realize the possibility within him. For to imagine and to shape the world is to *make ourselves responsible,* and responsibility *born of our freedom* can cause us to be afraid.

NOTES

Chapter II

1. *La Nausée,* p. 39.
2. *La Nausée,* p. 77.
3. *La Nausée,* pp. 47-48.
4. *Ibid.,* p. 153.
5. *La Nausée,* p. 42.
6. *L'Etre et le Néant,* p. 81.
7. *La Nausée,* p. 15.
8. *Ibid.,* p. 79.
9. *La Nausée,* p. 21.
10. *Ibid.,* p. 42.
11. *Ibid.,* pp. 23-24.
12. *La Nausée,* p.23.
13. *Ibid.,* p. 167.
14. *La Nausée,* p. 167.
15. *Ibid.,* p. 150.
16. *Ibid.,* p. 164.
17. *La Nausée,* pp. 165-166.
18. *Situations* I, p. 154.
19. *La Nausée,* p. 30.

20. *La Nausée*, pp. 131-132.

21. Rainer Maria Rilke, *Cahiers de Malte Laurids Brigge*, p. 108.

22. André Malraux, *La Voie royale*, pp. 262-263.

23. *La Nausée*, p. 87.

24. *Ibid.*, p. 60.

25. *Situations* I, p. 19.

26. Jean Anouilh, *Médée, Nouvelles Pièces noires*, p. 393.

27. *La Nausée*, p. 112.

28. *Ibid.*

29. *La Nausée*, p. 126.

30. Julien Green, *Si j'étais vous . . .* , p. 159.

31. Miguel de Unamuno, *Sentimiento trágico de la vida, Obras* (ed. Aguilar, Madrid, 1942) , II, 1171.

32. *L'Imaginaire*, p. 23.

33. *L'Etre et le Néant*, p. 28.

34. *L'Imagination*, p. 1.

35. *L'Etre et le Néant*, p. 43.

36. Cf. Spinoza: "Any determination entails negation." ("*Omnis determinatio est negatio.*")

37. *L'Etre et le Néant*, p. 61.

38. *Ibid.*, p. 58.

39. *L'Imagination*, p. 69.

40. *Situations* I, p. 32.

41. *Le Sursis*, p. 285.

42. *Le Sursis*, p. 285.

43. *La Nausée*, p. 21.

44. *Le Sursis*, p. 285.

45. *Le Sursis*, pp. 286-287.

46. *Baudelaire*, p. 33.

47. *Le Diable et le Bon Dieu*, pp. 171-172.

48. *Les Mains sales*, p. 111.

49. *Situations* I, p. 185.

50. *Les Mouches, Théâtre*, p. 102.

51. *La Nausée*, pp. 159-160.

52. *Morts sans sépulture, Théâtre*, p. 189.

53. *Les Mouches, Théâtre*, p. 98.

54. *Baudelaire*, p. 47.

55. *L'Age de raison*, p. 125.

56. *Le Sursis*, p. 286.

III. THE FEARS OF MEN

A. AGAINST HUMAN COMEDIES

Human existence has the unique function of creating the meaning of life. But man can not simply create this meaning once and for all and cling to it thereafter; he must on the contrary constantly renew it and assume it. By virtue of the very definition of consciousness, which is perpetual lucidity and continuous choice, life entails unrelenting effort.

Man tries to elude his responsibiliy. Because his life is not automatically justified but must be justified again and again, he seeks refuge in less demanding pursuits, in the rejection of creativity, and in the imitation of a *ready-made model*. On this point Sartre assumes once more the critical and rebellious attitude of his contemporaries and his predecessors; he shares in their intolerance and their scorn for "those corpses who would subject their life to a model." [1]

His whole psychology is grounded on the study of subterfuges, instances of "bad faith" through which man refuses to come face to face with his harsh destiny. Because it is distressing always to assume responsibility and to be constantly on the alert, man prefers to mask the obligation imposed by his freedom by imagining himself not as a being that ceaselessly creates new significations but as a fixed existence, unchangeable and recognized by others and by public opinion as an indisputable and reassuring value.

Man is faced with the *difficulty of existing,* this is *his situation* and this is what Roquentin feels in anguish. To cope with it, man must never cease willing and choosing; he must be forever renewing, forever free. Rather than make the requisite exertion most men prefer to *fashion a definite image of themselves,* to see themselves congealed into a stable existence.

Sartre analyzed this attitude in Baudelaire, who made himself an outcast in order *to be something* irrevocable, to cease questioning himself:

> He is the man who, most acutely aware of his human predicament, sought most avidly to hide it from himself. Since his "nature" escaped him, he tried to ensnare it in the eyes of others.[2]

Like a child who has an urge to assert too soon his personality and his existence and who, unable to do so normally, becomes rebellious and takes pleasure in constructing an image of himself which though unpleasant will at least "be," Baudelaire by opening the door to criticism and making himself an outcast creates the illusion of an existence otherwise denied him; unable to justify his own existence, he makes himself an object of scandal for others, and that is how he at last exists and breaks the bonds of anguish.

> All his life this man was incited by vanity and by spite *to become something* in his own eyes

and in the eyes of others. He wanted to set himself apart from the great social comedy and to stand erect like a statue, solid, opaque, unique. In short, he wanted *to be*.[3]

"To be of stone, immobile, insensible . . . with no project, no anxiety" [4] is man's dream. And Sartre condemns as base the dream of no longer being a free man obliged always to make decisions on his own but a definite, petrified, irresponsible thing. As one of Pirandello's heroines had put it earlier:

> What I want is to get away from myself, to remember nothing, nothing . . . to empty myself of my whole life . . . to look only at my body . . . *to be nothing more than this body*.[5]

We all want to fashion for ourselves a "personality"—a set of conventions, attitudes, and habits which define us in such a way that we need not bother "to exist" so long as we are faithful to the general pattern that we have set once and for all. Such is the petrification sought by most men and supported by their behavior, social considerations, and the comedies that they perform for themselves and for others.

* * *

For to fashion a personality with a minimum of effort on our part we need others. In their eyes we see ourself not as an unstable being forced always to decide what he will do the next second but as a thing which has its own traits and characteristics and which exists independently. According to Sartre our life often consists of "posing," of exhibiting ourselves to others not through superficial vanity but because the image that they fashion of us from without seems like a solid reality which can reassure us concerning ourselves and keep us from having to exert ourselves. There is a certain pleasure in "being seen" and therefore in feeling that we are "somebody"; we try to make ourselves important in the eyes of others because it is easier to do this than to obtain the approbation of our conscience. "Thus we escape anguish by trying to apprehend ourselves *from without* as we would the Other or a thing." [6] We prefer to imagine ourselves as other people see us rather than to question ourselves concerning what we really are. One of the characters in *No Exit* puts it this way:

> "There were six big mirrors in my bedroom. Whenever I talked, I would be in a position where I could watch myself in one of them. As I talked I could see myself talking. I saw myself as other people see me, and that kept me awake." [7]

Such is the import of the play, first performed in 1944, in which Sartre brought three people together in hell only to show how everyone needs others in order to create his own illusion of himself. Why hell, here represented quite simply by a provincial hotel room, without windows or mirrors and with only three couches for the three outcasts? Because *really* to exist man must be able to *will*, to project himself into the future and modify its signification. Estelle, Inès and Garcin are condemned to a false existence, to the existence which many men in this life unfortunately find satisfactory. Garcin, who is dead in hell, fears that his death was cowardly. He would like for this not to be true, but the only means of disproving it would be to give proof of his courage; since he is dead, however, he can no longer *do* anything. He therefore has recourse to a subterfuge in common use among the living; he tries to assure himself that he is not a coward by building in Estelle's eyes an image of himself as a valiant man, by not appearing to be a coward. This suggests a new insight into the eternal satire involving "being" and "appearing." In the same way Inès says to Estelle:

> "Come on now! You will be whatever you wish—spring water, filthy water, *you will see yourself in my eyes as you wish to see yourself.*" [8]

What other people offer us (and this is why we are so direly in need of them and the social comedy) is a reassuring image of ourselves. But this image is at bottom a lie which we implore of the Other and which we even impose on him by posing for him and deceiving him. But if the Other rejects this role, then he becomes our tormentor: "No brimstone is necessary; hell is other people." [9] Estelle in the end thrusts back on Garcin the responsibility which he seeks to unload on her:

> *Garcin*: Estelle, am I a coward?
> *Estelle*: Why I don't know, darling. *I am not in your skin. You have to decide that for yourself.*[10]

The last sentence sums up what has been said up to this point about Sartre's moral philosophy and at

65

the same time reveals his theory of psychology, which is the study of the poses that we assume and the comedies that we enact in the presence of the Other in order to avoid having to decide for ourselves. In *Roads to Freedom* Jacques Delarue, Mathieu's brother, had fled from Paris in June of 1940; later, however, thinking himself strong and energetic, he enacts this comedy in the presence of his wife Odette in order *to be told by her that he was not afraid*:

> He drew near her and said forcefully, as if to convince her, "There was no danger."
> She did not reply. He continued, softly but insistently, "I am sure that the Germans have good intentions. I know that they will behave themselves."
> That was what she had always thought. But in Jacques' eyes she could read the reply that he was expecting. She said, "Do we ever know for sure? Suppose they burned and ravaged Paris?"
> He shrugged. "Why should they? That's a woman's way of looking at it." [11]

Jacques resorts to all the basest and most inane subterfuges to force Odette to assure him that he did not act cowardly.

> Jacques' eyes sparkled. "If there had been any danger, I'd have stayed. I decided to leave only because I was sure that there was no danger."
> She remembered how he had entered the room, quiet and tense, the way his hand had

trembled when he lit his cigarette, his delib-
erate tone. "Pack your things, Odette. The car
is downstairs. We are leaving in thirty min-
utes." What did he expect her to do? He
laughed unpleasantly.[12]

Through his insistence he subjects his wife to psychological torture, trying to wrest from her the words
which will bring calm to the man who exists only
in the judgment of the Other and who is "posing."

He effected a virile and lonely smile, then
took her hand and said reassuringly. "What
could have happened to me, anyway? At the
worst, they may send the able-bodied men to
Germany. Even if they do, Mathieu will be all
right. He doesn't have my bad heart. You remember when that idiotic army doctor turned
me down?"
"Yes."
"I lost my head, remember? I was ready to
do just about anything to get in. Do you remember how upset I was?" [13]

Jacques is guilty of cowardice on two counts, since,
having been frightened, he thinks only of saving
face. True courage would consist of recognizing his
past fear and in behaving differently in the future.
But the image that others have of him matters more
to him than reality, and in this tendency to flee from
his inner responsibility and substitute for it an outer
semblance Sartre sees man's basic defect.
Concern over the Other, the mirror in which human weakness seeks a reflection of itself which will

exempt it from really being itself, is for Sartre the illusion that fascinates mankind. Bathed in the Other's look, we become at last a hard solid *object* and cease being an interrogation and an effort.

> The look of Medusa congeals and petrifies. Baudelaire can not complain, for the function of the Other's look is to transform him into a *thing*.[14]

If we do not wish to assume in its totality our responsibility to be a freedom and not a conventional appearance, we are compelled to pose, like Rirette in "Intimacy," and to imagine ourselves only as we are seen by the Other.

> They both laughed and passers-by turned to look back at them. Rirette thought that they must be charming to look at and was sorry that they were not sitting on the terrace of Viel or of the Café de la Paix.[15]

Here we have a prime example of a young woman who is concerned over her pose, under which there is nothing.

The Wall, published in 1939, is made up of a series of attitudes concerning the way in which man escapes his destiny by calling in the Other's look, *by asking the Other through the pleasing image that he reflects to serve as a substitute for an inner justification more difficult to achieve.* This book, in which Sartre evokes all the clamminess of intimacy, reveals man in the sheer nakedness of his artifices. Not, as one might think, because certain scenes are in themselves offensive but because the characters in these short stories are studied from a particular angle. They exist only because they play a role, not because they exercise their freedom. They are either sadists or masochists, that is, men who need others to make them suffer or who need to inflict suffering on others in order to create for themselves the illusion of finding a meaning in their existence. "He didn't want *me*," observes Rirette.

> "He wanted a *wife of his own*. That is why he married me and why he is my husband." [16]

Similarly, Inès states in *No Exit*:

> "I'm wicked. This means that I need the suffering of others in order to exist." [17]

It would be entirely correct to say that these characters are monsters, but what writer has not drawn on monsters to illustrate his thought? And his monstrosity is but an exaggerated symbol of the temptation of bad faith (self-deception) which, according to Sartre, poisons man. Man is tempted to justify his existence by cruelly imposing on others some sort of definite image of himself, and even, in the absence of anything else, one that is brutal and obscene. And Sartre deemed it necessary to deal with its extreme forms, sadism and masochism, in order to illuminate the temptation of bad faith.

The main thing is to be seen—to appear in order not to have to be. Daniel Sereno wishes always to have the feeling that "someone" is looking at him and making him exist, that he is "something" for

69

"someone." If he believes that he is seen by God, he will be able to accept himself, to have the impression of being and of no longer questioning himself:

> Above all, to stop looking at myself, for when I look at myself I am double. *To be*. In the darkness, groping about. To be a pederast as the oak is an oak. To die away. To snuff out the inner look.[18]

God's look will then confer on him changeless qualities and he will no longer have to bother about what he is, since the Other sees him and makes him be:

> "Lord, I *am* a miser. And the petrifying look of Medusa will fall down on him from above. Stone virtues, stone vices. How comforting."[19]

Obviously, of course, Christianity neither postulates nor condones such acceptance of the self and requires on the contrary that the old man be cast out in order that to some degree life may be illuminated.

But here Sartre is pointing up the necessity of avoiding the perpetual invention of the self and the world, which is at the heart of consciousness. In short, man, to avoid making the effort of being a project that is unceasingly renewed, cravenly aspires to being his own statue.

That is why he so often plays a role. By identifying ourselves with an image which we construct mainly for others, we assume an easy role. Habit and routine rather than vanity may motivate us; we choose the gestures appropriate to our profession and our position, and we repeat them automatically. The result is our mien, our self-assurance, our smugness—in brief, everything that has a part in the little game we play as if we were looking affably at ourselves in a mirror. Every man plays a role in this comedy:

> Take the bartender. A moment ago he had been smoking a cigarette, as indifferent and poetic as a bindweed; now he had roused himself and was a little too much the bartender; he rattled the shaker, opened it, poured a foaming yellow liquid into the glasses with movements which were just a little too precise. He was playing at being a bartender.[20]

The bartender's game had already been described much earlier in *Being and Nothingness*:

> Consider the waiter. His movements are quick and sure, a little too precise, a little too fast. He comes toward the customers a little too quickly, bends over a little too eagerly; his voice, his eyes express a little too much concern over the client's order; finally we see him coming back, trying to imitate in his walk the inflexible rigidity of some imaginary automaton and carrying his platter with the daring of a funambulist, continuously throwing it off-balance and continuously restoring its delicate equilibrium with the slight movement of his arm and hand.[21]

Thus the exercising of our most familiar functions is transformed into a series of gestures and attitudes which we have formed once and for all.

71

He is playing a role, having a good time. But what role is he playing? It is not necessary to observe him long to realize that he is *playing at being a waiter*.[22]

In every role we find the artifice which confronts and ensnares man:

> This obligation does not differ from that imposed on all businessmen. Their comportment is wholly ceremonial; the public requires them to act out their parts. The grocer, the tailor, the auctioneer — each has his dance through which he takes pains to persuade his clients that he is nothing other than a grocer, a tailor, or an auctioneer.[23]

Instead of actually living his life, man generally acts out a part just as the man in the street plays a part in the presence of his wife. As Sartre puts it:

> The attentive pupil who wants *to be* attentive, his eyes riveted on the teacher, his ears bent on hearing every word, becomes so exhausted as a result of playing at being attentive that finally he no longer hears anything.[24]

Instead of accepting our spontaneity and controlling it, we insist on wanting *to be* something; and the pretense at being which we assume is a comedy. All that is needed to bring out the comic element in human poses is to find ourselves in exceptional circumstances like the condemned man in *The Wall*:

The other officer indolently raised his pale hand. His indolence was also contrived. I could see through all their little schemes and was astounded that any man could amuse himself in such a way.[25]

Often the game involves only social prestige. But what is behind it all?

The man who is brought into the room is the gynecologist, formerly an intern in Paris, and a major in World War I. Take away the doctor, take away the major, and all that is left is a little dirty water swirling through a cesspool.[26]

These things, though certainly not expressed in elegant terms, are designed to focus attention on the naked truth. For there is an element of sincerity in the acceptance of the human comedy which obscures the pharisaism that makes us label men in defiance of the brute facts:

A family man is never a true family man. An assassin is never an assassin in every respect. They are play-acting. Do you understand? [27]

Even robbers "*play* at being robbers." [28]

Concerning man in such a situation, Sartre says that he "gets stuck" or "is infected with viscosity" because he clings to a factitious appearance instead of being a perpetually renewed creation of himself. The sight of the quasi-comedy played by man terrifies him and gives him a peculiar feeling of disgust.

Erostrate in *The Wall* expresses the extreme form of this feeling, for he professes to hate men:

> I tell you that *I can't love them.* I understand clearly what you feel. But what you find appealing in them disgusts me. Like you I've seen men masticating rhythmically even as they peruse a scholarly journal, using the left hand to turn the pages. Is it my fault if I prefer to watch the seals feed? The slightest facial movement of man becomes a physiognomic game.[29]

Duhamel had previously depicted this grotesque spectacle in *Salavin's Journal* and in *Confession at Midnight*: he attributed to Salavin the same susceptibility in this respect as does Sartre to Erostrate. But that is not the crucial issue. The social comedy persists in spite of its ridiculous side, and we continue to play a role for ourselves and for others, as Mathieu observes:

> Maybe you can't do anything else; maybe you have to choose whether to be nothing or to play at being what you are. That would be terrible . . . the dice would be loaded.[30]

* * *

What is here rejected by Sartre (and obviously also by most of his contemporaries) are the conventions of civilization. In short, the man who as the waiter plays the part of a waiter or who as a lawyer plays the part of a lawyer is merely agreeing to conform to the general pattern laid out for him.

The man who develops a certain attitude does so because in his relation with the Other it epitomizes what he represents. It is socially appropriate for the waiter to be solicitous, for the doctor to evidence a complacent and authoritative air which will comfort the patient and his family. In sum, these little comedies have been tacitly adopted because they are useful.

They are false, to be sure, and insincere. The waiter may well damn inwardly the customer to whom he is outwardly solicitous, the doctor may diagnose authoritatively even when he himself understands nothing about the case before him. The problem is to determine the efficiency of conventions. The social lie is obviously an evil, and it would be desirable to have the doctor, lawyer, and bartender play their roles without having recourse to it; it would be commendable, in view of Sartre's emphasis on the necessity toward oneself, if actions, instead of being predicated on habits and attitudes, were on the contrary always "natural" in Stendhal's sense of the word—if they were never stereotyped but always spontaneous. And this quality is found in a few individuals; we speak of natural abilities, a natural comedian, etc. But men who measure up to Sartre's standard of sincerity possess unusual lucidity; they never fall back upon patterned actions, and they have a *new approach to each circumstance*. The ideal is seductive, and Stendhal had already formulated it, applying it to what he called "the select few" or "noble natures." But each man's resistance is limited and probably predictable. Instead of evidencing a fresh, sincere attitude when he comes to his fiftieth case, the doctor besieged by patients may have recourse to conventional complacency, to ready-made gestures, even to pat expressions, and the bartender unnerved by impolite customers may adopt a smug attitude toward them; their actions, though obviously deplorable, are nevertheless inevitable. Sartre feels that in adopting a conventional attitude they are abdicating their freedom and their spontaneity. Still, in so doing they are *choosing*, and generally quite lucidly, to have recourse at the end of the day to an automatism which will enable them to have strength on the following day to be more natural and more sincere. And has Sartre himself never at the end of a lecture given banal, stereotyped answers to questions in order that he might profitably take them up again the next day? [31]

Our civilization and its fixed values, through the conventional attitudes that they afford for consolidating our efficiency and enabling us to discharge the duties of our profession with casual authoritativeness, allow us to have recourse in daily living to an "automatic pilot." When fair weather prevails, the pilot of a plane, in order to conserve his strength in case of a storm, may set in operation an automatic mechanism which will insure the stability of the plane under normal conditions; in the same way civilized living, in exchange for its complexity and the frequent adaptive efforts required of us, provides us with the faculty for living and thinking somewhat automatically whenever imperious necessity no longer commands our attention. Perpetual lucidity seems like a beautiful ideal and a requirement that might be formulated by a professor of philosophy, but studies in psychology and physiology would show that we can not endure maximal tension for twenty-four or even sixteen hours daily. It seems that in instituting customs, conventions, and patterns of living, civilization has unconsciously compensated for forcing us to expend an excessive amount of nervous energy by providing us with masks which we can use to achieve some measure of repose. If there were in the world but one bartender and but one genial customer, the bartender would always be natural and sincere in his relations with the customer; he would never be upset and would never substitute conventional services and professional gestures for spontaneous attentiveness. An ideal society of beings educated in lucidity would make possible mutual services and mutual trust; in the absence of such a society, the "confection" which Sartre deplores is inevitable. For our nervous tensions civilization offers periods of semi-automatic activity which, from the point of view of sincerity toward oneself, obviously bear the stamp of comedy and hypocrisy.

But inherent in the possibility of conventionality opened up by patterns of behavior and customs is the great danger that it will provide an alibi for laziness rather than for fatigue, for falsity rather than for spontaneity held in reserve. The masks made available by civilization and routine may and in practice often do cover up disloyal actions and attitudes. That is why Sartre's criticism of human comedies retains its bite and its validity. Because social convention is obviously a convenient mask, writers have the mission not so much of denouncing its abuses as of showing their relative importance. The literature of our age eloquently warns us against the danger of hypocrisy, and Sartre furnishes convincing proof of the importance of that danger.

B. SATIRE ON CONFORMITY

He thereby expresses the conflict which though doubtlessly eternal is especially acute in our age and to which throughout the centuries a goodly third of French literature has been devoted—the conflict between civilization and sincerity.

In our age particularly, André Gide is doubtlessly the initiator of the search for sincerity and the campaign to denounce social masks. "We live on convention," the Counterfeiters say.[32] Gide's contemporary, Pirandello, who also foresaw a crisis in the relation between social and individual sensibility, pointed to the same hiatus between sincerity and truth: "Often we are no more sincere toward ourselves than toward others." [33] And the great Italian dramatist not only focused attention on a psychological relativity long recognized as such but also stressed the artifice through which man constructs for himself a false coherence: "We are what we construct; that is the pivotal point of Pirandello's art." [34]

That man acts out a part had been noted by all of Sartre's predecessors. Take cowardice, singled out by Péguy; pretense, accepted as a matter of course, in a sense marks the death of sincerity. "Death is satiation—with pretense, with memory, with growing old. It is therefore satiation with sclerosis and with induration." [35] Thus Péguy adumbrated Sartre's concept of viscosity just as Gide had a presentiment of his definition of the spells cast by the Other's look. "Most of men's actions, even those not dictated by self-interest, are influenced by the Other's look, by vanity, by fashion ... " [36]

Or take social masks. Here Jean Anouilh was very close to Sartre when he had Ludovic say in *Y avait un prisonnier*:

> "I consent to every kind of filthiness! Vice is nothing; the farce that it creates is what makes life terrifying."

The last sentence probably justifies all the apparent immorality in "Intimacy," one of the short stories in *The Wall*.

Thus Sartre, as a scholastic concerned with satire, lends support to a movement which had its beginning in the past and which contests in the name of sincerity the false coherence to which human life has recourse.

The very idea of personality is then called in question—a normal reaction against several centuries of "character delineation" and "analysis of the passions," against the nineteenth century during which this tendency had managed to congeal in the description of social types. This vision of man entailed as a logical reaction the notion of freedom through which the individual ceases to be subjected to a ready-made coherence which is his character, to specific traits which define him socially. And for Sartre as well as for Gide, the *opposition between sincerity and imposture* takes on an ethical aspect. He would have man reject imposture and be freedom.

* * *

The study of bad faith (self-deception) in man turns up the secret or social comedies through which everyone seeks to congeal in a predetermined and obligingly contrived personage. In this search for alibis and in this masked ball, *social conformity* plays a role. To "respected citizens," to those who are important and those who are self-centered, it offers a purely formal life characterized by smugness and haughtiness, by acquired routines and ideas.

Such are the citizens of Bouville observed by Roquentin:

"I feel so far away from them, up on the top of this hill. It seems as if I belong to another species. They come out of their offices after their day's work, they look at the houses and squares with satisfaction, they think that it is *their* town—a good, middle-class town. They are not afraid, they feel at home. All they have ever seen is tame water running from a spigot, light that pours into bulbs when a switch is flipped, mongrel, bastard trees held up by props. They prove, a hundred times a day, that everything happens mechanically, that the world obeys fixed, immutable laws. Bodies falling freely through a void all travel at the same rate of speed, the public park closes daily at 4 p.m. in winter, at 6 p.m. in summer, lead melts at 335 degrees centigrade, the last streetcar leaves the Hôtel de Ville at 11:05 p.m. They are peaceable, a little morose; they think about Tomorrow, that is, another today; cities have at their disposal but one day, and every morning it comes back exactly the same. They do brighten it a little on Sundays. Idiots. I hate to think that I'm going to see their thick, smug faces again." [37]

Here Sartre satirizes not only the routines that make up civilization—for it is after all absolutely necessary for the last streetcar to leave at 11:05 p.m. —but also men who are satisfied with these routines, who accept them as justification for existence, who (as Bernanos would say) *substitute a banal, superficial order for the spiritual life.* By creating a sort of self-satisfaction and a sham social life, they bring about hypocrisy. Man may at times feel the poverty of conventional values but when he finds himself alone, unarmed, empty, he has recourse to them and wallows in them as does Odette Delarue. Though she has seen through the pathetic little comedies of her husband, too weak to come to grips with the piercing question of the meaning of existence, she needs his assurance:

> She was afraid; he was sleeping and she had again found the dark world of her childhood, the forest of unanswered questions. *He* knew the names of the stars, the number of inhabitants of the region, their history and their occupations; he is asleep, and I hate him and I know nothing; she felt lost in this futile world, in this world created *to be seen and touched.* She ran back to the car, eager to awaken him at once, to awaken Science, Industry, Ethics. [38]

The net result is that conventional values create for us a make-believe world, a world in which fears

81

are transformed into certainties and pretenses. We are then induced to solve the problem of living, not through an interrogation of our conscience and a personal commitment of our responsibility, but through reverence, obeisance, and admiration with respect to values which often are only conventions and lies, like the proud reverent citizens of Bouville in the presence of the statue erected in honor of the great man of their city:

> The holy ideas, the good ideas that they have from their fathers, they are no longer responsible for defending; a man of bronze has become their guardian.[39]

By practicing conformity, rather than by assuming a personal risk and being ourselves, we relegate the responsibility for our acts to a penal and moral code. We need only follow it or merely give lip service to it and then relax with a clear conscience. This is the epitome of the pharisaical attitude: "They knew it. They knew that they were right and that God, if he existed, was on their side." [40]

This purely collective and formal moral code, which excludes all inner responsibility and the whole "spiritual life" [41] is obviously devoid of sincerity. It is counterfeit; it glosses over the hypocrisy and the short-comings of the powerful. That is what Sartre emphasizes in *The Respectful Prostitute,* the play in which he transports to the United States his satire of morality based on purely social considerations. Here a woman of ill repute, by nature sincere and spontaneous, is the victim of an attack on the part of the son of a reputable family. Since

82

it would obviously be impossible to admit that one of the future pillars of society could be guilty, the crime is attributed to a poor innocent Negro. As a simple-minded person with a naive respect for truth, the courtesan at first wishes to reconstruct the facts and to testify correctly. But there are attempts to persuade her that truth and justice are always on the side of respectable people and that the wellborn son *must* be innocent:

> *Senator*: Do you believe that a whole town can be wrong? A whole town with its ministers and priests, its lawyers and artists, its mayor and city fathers and its charitable organizations? Do you believe that? [42]

The Senator goes even further. Though he recognizes the facts, to falsify them he invokes *social utility* which then becomes the driving force behind their counterfeit morality. The black man is nothing and is good for nothing. It is obvious that the white man has done something bad and that he is really the guilty one. "But I need him," says the Senator.

> "He is one hundred percent American, the scion of one of our oldest families, a Harvard graduate, an officer—I need officers—he employs two thousand workers in his factory—two thousand unemployed if he should die. . . . It is his duty to live and it is your duty to save his life. That's the way things stand. Now choose." [43]

Between threats and bribery are many means of forcing a lie from a poor girl whose situation is insecure; the courtesan then reluctantly becomes respectful, no longer toward justice, but toward people in high positions; and Sartre goes a step further and shows that after obtaining her perjured testimony, they do not even bother to pay her or to thank her.

In fact, values mask hypocrisy for the reason that the individual, because he fears existence, is hard put to justify himself. Unable unceasingly to re-create his own values or even to quicken within himself, sincerely and authentically, values that already exist, he takes refuge in false values and uses them as a mask. In the eternal quarrel between those who say that evil has its source in an unjust society and those who believe that it is inherent in man, Sartre, in spite of appearances and in spite of the stress that he places on satirizing society, seems to belong to the second group. For him social values are unauthentic because the individual has recourse to hypocritical conventions through fear of having to assume and be solely responsible for his own values.

That is indeed Lucien Fleurier's odyssey in "Childhood of a Leader," a story which appeared in *The Wall* (1938) and which, along with *Nausea*, is probably Sartre's masterwork. Lucien Fleurier is destined to become a leader to succeed his father, an industrialist with a high position in society; this entails developing unqualified respect for established values and becoming a prisoner of prejudices. But Sartre tries to discover how Lucien becomes this congealed person. Like all children, though less lucidly than Roquentin, Lucien sometimes glimpses the gratuitous nature of existence. Upbraided for being duped, he begins to wonder about himself:

Who am I? I look at my desk, I look at my notebook. My name is Lucien Fleurier, but that is not a name. I'm wrong. I'm right. I don't know. It makes no sense.[44]

He would like to "be" but, still sincere, he does not know what he is. *He* would have to decide, but that would require that supreme human effort, and we know that he will later prefer to fall back upon a ready-made model.

His first years, those of a typical middle-class child, are described with gentle irony. Still not committed to the game of conventions, he feels that life, and even the life of adults, is often counterfeit and constitutes a game. His parents adopt attitudes and he does not know how to play his part:

> Mama was playing at being tormented because her little jewel ate so little; Papa was playing at reading the newspaper and at shaking his finger in Lucien's face from time to time and saying, "Badaboom, little fellow!" And Lucien was also playing at something, only he did not know exactly what it was.[45]

Adolescence brings its difficulties, its experiences, a certain self-consciousness, and an awareness of his awkwardness:

> Lucien did not know what to do with his body; no matter what he set out to do, he always had the impression that his body was existing simultaneously in all directions, without asking his advice.[46]

All during his awkward development Lucien is well aware of his desire *to assume a definite shape.* But how? He will not hesitate to adopt the easiest means—ready-made attitudes. He begins to admire his cocksure comrade:

> Gary, for example, did not exist any more than Lucien. But it was enough to see him snort rakishly when surrounded by his admirers; it was immediately apparent that he was absolutely certain of his own existence.[47]

Then, enrolled in the preparatory class at Central, he feels himself a part of the warm universe of the collective life and traditions of higher education, free to assume an importance in a world equipped with organized scandals:

> At such times Lucien felt galvanized. In the evening he would give his parents a detailed account of the diverse incidents of the day, and when he said, "Then the whole class burst out laughing," or "We all decided to give Meyrinez the silent treatment," his words as they came out warmed his mouth like a drink of alcohol.[48]

Finally he meets comrades who have political convictions and sees in them a means of making himself feel important. Without realizing that he is still "playing," he assumes certain attitudes and proclaims certain opinions:

> He enjoyed a few successes and when he said concerning Herriot, "If that man dies in his bed, there is no such thing as a good Lord," he

experienced a feeling of righteous indignation. Then he gritted his teeth and for a moment felt *just as convinced, just as rigid, just as erect, just as powerful* as Rémy or Desperreau. "Lemordant is right," he thought. "Everything comes with experiences." [49]

He seeks conviction, rigidity, power, even if they must be artificial. He garbs himself in the bad taste, prejudices, and affectations of society, and the day he causes a scandal in the presence of a rival and thereby affirms his position, in the false respect accorded him he sees clearly what he has gained in the eyes of others. "My parents say that you were right," admits his friend, "that you could act in no other way once you have a 'conviction.' " [50] From that moment he is possessed by the idea of a petrified Order in which everyone has his place in society and thinks himself sufficiently justified by his external role:

He thought for a moment, serious and pious, and the words came spontaneously. "I have my rights! My rights! Something on the order of triangles and circles. Something so perfect that it does not exist. It would be pointless to make thousands of rings with a compass; one could never create a single circle." In the same way. generations of workers might scrupulously obey Lucien's orders and yet never succeed to his right to command; rights, like mathematical objects and religious dogmas, transcend existence. And that described perfectly Lucien: a huge complex of rights and responsibilities.[51]

Thus Evil is for Sartre the burning desire *to be* something solid and unchangeable, to make oneself a social object that has only an artificial existence. Lucien Fleurier has become a hard, petrified man, and all his past worries, though indistinctly illuminated by nascent but still unseen freedom, have become for him as for Jacques Delarue merely an alibi for a personal reassessment:

> Jacques was very proud of his youth; it was his guarantee. It allowed him to defend the existing order with a clear conscience. For five years he had studiously aped every deviation that came into vogue; he had fallen into surrealism as well as into a few flattering relationships, and he had at times sniffed a handkerchief dipped in ethyl chloride before making love. Then he had settled down: Odette's dowry amounted to six hundred thousand francs. He had written to Mathieu, "You have to have the courage to act like everybody to avoid being like nobody." And he had set up a law office.[52]

Strictly in accordance with the illusions of our age, social values, those bulwarks of sacred rights that mask hypocrisy and those haughty disguises of the weak, are looked upon as an easy way out for those who wish to hide from themselves the fact that life would require of them solutions that are perpetually to be found anew and, even more important, a strictly individual responsibility; for that is frequently what Sartre means by "commitment":

> Every man has made a commitment, but that does not mean that he is fully aware of it; most

men devote all their time to dissembling their commitment.[53]

Such men have recourse to conventions, and literature itself can be at fault whenever its goal is nothing more than seemliness, whenever it is merely

> . . . enthralled talent turned against itself, the art of using harmonious and innocuous words to banish fears, to show in a cavalier fashion that the world and man are transparent, mediocre, and devoid of surprises, threats, and interests.[54]

Sartre dwells at length on that point in *What Is Literature?* He insists that literature should not be devoted exclusively to conventional artifices but should have an unmistakable and untarnished meaning.

It is only by apprehending the originality of his own destiny, without recourse to the comedy of pretenses, that man will be a true man. Most men let themselves sink into prepared molds like soft dough; whoever resists being trapped by artifice then feels hard and clean:

> "Brunet put on his jacket. He felt clean, fresh and stiff. His face was aglow." [55]

Or again:

> "I was terribly hard at that instant, and I wanted to stay hard." [56]

As early as 1938 in *Nausea* and to an even greater degree in 1939 in *The Wall,* Sartre had satirized the comic situations that involve self-deception as well as those that involve conformity; these became constant themes in his later works, some of which were to be expected: *The Age of Reason* and *The Reprieve* (1945), *No Exit* (1945), and *The Respectful Prostitute* (1946).

Against this, and in a positive sense, the possibility of avoiding self-deception and vulgar conformity is dealt with as early as 1943 in *The Flies* and, beginning in 1945, in *Roads to Freedom*.

NOTES

Chapter III

1. Malraux, *La Voie Royale*, p. 54.
2. *Baudelaire*, p. 47.
3. *Ibid.*, p. 90.
4. *Le Sursis*, p. 107.
5. Pirandello, *Comme tu me veux, Théâtre* II, p. 48.
6. *L'Etre et le Néant*, p. 81.
7. *Huis-clos, Théâtre*, p. 136.
8. *Huis-clos, Théâtre*, p. 154.
9. *Ibid.*, p. 167.
10. *Huis-clos, Théâtre*, p. 158.
11. *La Mort dans l'âme*, p. 160.
12. *Ibid.*, p. 161.
13. *La Mort dans l'âme*, pp. 161-162.
14. *Baudelaire*, p. 137.
15. *Le Mur*, p. 113.
16. *Ibid.*, p. 125.
17. *Théâtre*, p. 144.
18. *Le Sursis*, p. 107.
19. *Ibid.*, p. 158.

20. *L'Age de raison*, p. 181.
21. *L'Etre et le Néant*, pp. 98-99.
22. *Ibid.*, p. 99.
23. *L'Etre et le Néant*, p. 99.
24. *Ibid.*, p. 100.
25. *Le Mur*, p. 31.
26. *Situations* I, p. 218.
27. *Les Mains sales*, p. 169.
28. *Saint-Genêt, comedien et martyr*, p. 121.
29. *Le Mur*, p. 80.
30. *L'Age de raison*, p. 181.
31. In contrast to the usual brilliance of his thinking, the whole lecture published under the title of *L'Existentialisme est un humanisme* consists of platitudes, and I believe that Sartre has openly acknowledged this fact.
32. André Gide, *Les Faux-Monnayeurs* II, 136.
33. Pirandello, *Les trois pensées de la petite bossue*, p. 28.
34. Andrien Tilgher, *Relativistes contemporains*, p. 81.
35. Péguy, *Oeuvres* IX, p. 117.
36. Gide, *Journal*, p. 1054.
37. *La Nausée*, p. 204.
38. *La Mort dans l'âme*, p. 164.
39. *La Nausée*, p. 45.
40. *L'Age de raison*, p. 143.
41. It is wrong to use this expression drawn from the lexicon of Christianity in connection with Sartre. But since he has not yet published his *Ethics*, he has not created a vocabulary of his own. He has nevertheless, as Francis Jeanson has shown, used the term "purifying reflection," but in such a casual context that it has not been popularized like the other terms in his vocabulary.
42. *La Putain Respectueuse, Théâtre*, pp. 283-284.
43. *Ibid.*, p. 282.
44. *Le Mur*, p. 157.
45. *Le Mur*, p. 139.
46. *Ibid.*, p. 152.
47. *Ibid.*, p. 158.
48. *Le Mur*, p. 161.
49. *Ibid.*, p. 206.
50. *Ibid.*, p. 216.

51. *Ibid.*, p. 220.
52. *L'Age de raison*, p. 114.
53. *Situations* II, pp. 123-124.
54. *Ibid.*, pp. 157-158.
55. *La Mort dans l'âme*, p. 198.
56. *Le Mur*, p. 22.

IV. THE ODYSSEY OF FREEDOM

A. FROM ESTHETICISM TO ACTION

The Flies (1943) reflects the profound influence which the war, captivity, and the Resistance had on Sartre's thought. Until then he had insisted that individual freedom must not be masked and fettered by self-deception and social conformity, but he had advanced nothing, except perhaps watchful lucidity that ran the risk of remaining purely critical and negative if not actually vain, to serve as a guide in the pursuit of his ideal; we can never be certain that we are not playing a role, and even as we say to ourselves, "I will not assume a conventional attitude," there is nothing to guarantee that we will stop being comedians.

The criterion will then be *the degree of personal responsibility that we put into our acts*. If the demands made on us commit us in such a way that we incur a risk, our conduct will bear the stamp of authenticity to the extent that we accept the consequences of our actions.

Such is the transformation of young Oreste during the play. Educated in the tradition of comfortable living, irresponsibility, and estheticism, far from his own family and yet responsible for avenging his

father's death, he wants only to hold on to his in-
decisive position and refuses to take a stand. His
pedagogue had brought him up in such a way as to
allow him to enjoy life even while remaining uncommitted.

> "Now you are young, rich, and handsome, as cir-
> cumspect as an old man; you have no beliefs,
> no family, no country, no religion, no occupa-
> tion; you are free for any commitment and
> know that you must never commit yourself—in
> short, you are a superior man." [1]

But in this unsettled situation Oreste has an uneasy
feeling; nothing constrains him, but at the same
time nothing belongs to him; his freedom is empty
and he wonders if he is really living:

> "To love, to hate, is to give oneself up. He
> makes a fine impression, this aristocrat en-
> trenched in his worldly possessions, when one
> day he gives himself over to love, to hate, and
> with himself his land, his house, and his mem-
> ories." [2]

On returning at the age of twenty to the town of
Argos where he was born but about which he re-
members nothing, Oreste feels that he is cut off
from life. Men with *their* problems seem alien to
this stripling with none of his own. But while their
industry seemed grotesque to Roquentin, Oreste is
envious: "Oh, if only there were acts which would
give me the rights of a citizen among them." [3] For
Sartre has now discovered in human warmth and

solidarity ideas capable of giving a content, a practical application, and a field of action to freedom. To make contact with reality the man concerned with an abstract freedom must mingle with other men, enter into their quarrels, and transform the world by giving it the meaning that he has chosen. He must *act* and *choose*, but Oreste vacillates.

On learning of the crime that has been oppressing the town, he ought to try to seek revenge. But social conformity intervenes in the form of Jupiter, the king of the gods: Why punish a murderer twenty years after his crime has been committed? Why disturb the established order for the sake of an offense protected by the statute of limitations? This is also the crux of Giraudoux's *Electre,* borrowed from the same tragic Greek myth in which Oreste runs head on into the argument that influences the decision of Sartre's Oreste. He asks for a sign:

> "Zeus, I implore you, if resignation and abject humility are the laws that you impose on me, show your will through some sign." [4]

Then the Master of the Established Order makes the mistake of answering too obligingly and too quickly with a miracle; his facility reveals to Oreste the baseness of men. The make-believe god is but the image of their need for timorous tranquility; he is too easily persuaded by their fear and complacency.[5] Oreste cries out:

> "Then . . . is *that* the great Good? . . . Being submissive. Swallowing insults. Always saying 'I beg your Pardon,' and 'Thank you.' Is that what it is? The great Good. *Their great Good.*" [6]

He will not be a party to conformity which recommends that things always be left as they are; he discovers *that he himself can choose, at the price of his responsibility,* the shape which the world will assume for him:

> "But suddenly freedom spilled down on me and chilled me, nature took a backward leap, and I was no longer old, and I felt all alone in the middle of your benign little world, like someone who has lost his shadow; and there was no longer anything in heaven, neither Good nor Evil nor anyone to issue orders." [7]

And then he decides to avenge his father's death, no matter what the cost. But the essential thing is that Oreste discovers his freedom, that in resolving to *act,* to *commit an act on his own,* he learns that the greatness of man is in commitment, in his willingness to assume responsibility.

The notion that *the meaning of human life is man's responsibility* takes first place, from this time on, in Sartre's moral philosophy. While it is obvious that the same notion is common to most systems of ethics, even those furthest from Sartre's, his merit is in bringing it forcefully to the attention of human beings who adopt it in theory but take pains to forget about it in practice.

Roads to Freedom is the odyssey of a freedom still uncommitted, and Professor Mathieu Delarue lives through, more slowly and over a longer period, the same adventure as Oreste.

B. EMPTY FREEDOM

The first volume, *The Age of Reason*, begins in July, 1938. Its artistry resides in the rigorous realism of the cafe and the street, in the rather bleak life of the quasi-bohemians who people it, in their disabused and flippant, yet frank manner, in their boundless horizons, and in their style of living which border on baseness but which combat deception. Many of his admirers saw fit to try to copy the style of the work, even as Sartre himself was trying to go beyond it.

The Age of Reason begins with a street scene. A beggar accosts Mathieu and asks for a handout, intending to go immediately to a bistro for a drink:

> In the middle of the Rue Vercingétorix, a big fellow seized Mathieu by the arm; a policeman was walking his beat on the other sidewalk.
>
> "Give me something, boss. I'm hungry."
>
> His eyes were close together and his lips were thick. He reeked of alcohol.
>
> "You mean you are thirsty, don't you?" asked Mathieu.
>
> "No, I'm hungry. I swear it," he stammered. "I swear it."
>
> Mathieu had found a coin in his pocket. "Not that I really give a damn," he said. "I was just making conversation."
>
> He gave him the coin.[8]

In the face of Mathieu's generosity, the drunkard makes an attempt to shake off his torpor; he wants to show his appreciation and gives Delarue a stamp of which he is apparently fond, for it comes from

97

Madrid, where Spain is fighting. The beggar explains that he is a shirker but that he was almost a man, that he almost set out to fight in Spain. The episode is symbolic, for Mathieu goes away thinking that like the shirker, he has taken pains never to commit himself to an act that entails risk or responsibility. Now he has reached maturity but has not found a role, and during the oppressive and somewhat tarnished months of early summer in Paris, he wanders around with his empty freedom, his vain lucidity, contemplating like an indifferent but familiar visitor the sights of the Latin Quarter:

> . . . the Luxembourg, warm and white, statues and pigeons, children. The children run, the pigeons fly away. Races, white flashes, rank confusion.[9]

Or he stops to consider the adolescent prurience of lycée students in a cafe:

> Two young people had stopped near him; they were looking disdainfully at a table.
> "Sit down," said one of them, in English.
> "Je sit down," answered the other.
> They both laughed and sat down; their hands were dirty, their faces hard, and their flesh tender.
> "There are only crab lice in here!" thought Mathieu, irritated.[10]

Nothing determines his life; he does not want to be a *type foutu* with "a wife and five kids," and he is nothing. After he finishes his schooling, his sole distractions consist of paying court in an awkward way to the sister of a former pupil, a bantering eccentric named Ivich, and wrestling with the problem posed by the pregnancy of his mistress, Marcelle Duffet. The event provides whatever intrigue there is in the book, for Mathieu Delarue, faithful to his attitude of uncommitted freedom, does not wish to commit himself to a marriage, just as despite his convictions he did not go to Spain to fight.

He represents man aware of his freedom but unable to recognize its worth and interpret correctly its meaning; he wants to "conserve" it rather than to "commit" it. Boredom results:

> "Here I am, I taste myself, I sense the old taste of blood, and of chalybeate water, my taste, I'm my own taste, I exist. To exist is to imbibe oneself without thirst. Thirty-four. Thirty-four and I taste myself and I'm old. I've worked, I've waited, I've had what I wanted: Marcelle, Paris, independence; it's all over. I expect nothing more." [11]

Sartre has been criticized for his weak characters. But he recognizes their frailty without condoning it and, independently of his sympathy for them, needs to have recourse to them. Only the man who is mistaken concerning the meaning of freedom can show its true meaning. Contrast is necessary. A man who gave himself over wholly to freedom and thereby escaped frailty would prove nothing. Mathieu Delarue has to be mistaken concerning the organization of his life and *discover that something is lacking*; to bring to light the true meaning of life

Sartre must describe failures who will point up their short-comings. For Mathieu feels that he is a failure, *a man who through fear of losing his freedom has not put it to use*; he is "always the one who did not learn English, who did not join the Communist party, who did not go to Spain." [12] His situation is again that of Roquentin: "I am free. I no longer have a reason for living." [13] And ironically he contemplates the freedom which depends on its never being put to use, the freedom which is always held in reserve and which feeds on itself and is therefore empty and ineffectual, with the same bitterness that Oreste showed before his conversion in speaking to his tutor:

> "You have left me the freedom of threads which the wind tears from spiderwebs and wafts along ten feet above the ground; I weigh no more than a thread and I live in the air." [14]

Tired of always holding himself in reserve for an occasion that never arises, Mathieu is seized by jealousy in the presence of friends who have committed themselves and who therefore have a goal in life. They were not afraid of alienating their freedom, of sacrificing themselves to something other than themselves, and in exchange for their sacrifice, what they do has taken on a meaning. He looks enviously on Brunet who has become a militant politician:

> He had committed himself, he had renounced his freedom, he was no longer anything other than a soldier. And everything had been given back to him, even his freedom. He is freer than I am; he is at one with himself and with the Party.[15]

Brunet no longer has Mathieu's uneasiness: "He is completely calm now, he thinks: Wherever there are men, I have my place and my work." [16] The man who has committed himself has re-established contact with reality, like Oreste when he made his decision. When Mathieu lunches with Gomez the combatant, he feels that Gomez is truly alive:

> The steaks are on the table; one for him, one for me. He has the right to relish his, he has the right to tear into it with his beautiful white teeth, he has the right to look at the pretty girl on his left and to think, "a nice piece." I don't have. If I eat, a hundred dead Spaniards will jump at my throat. I haven't paid.[17]

The theme will be taken up again and again in later works. In *Dirty Hands* Jessica, a flighty woman, recognizes the reality and the virility of Hoederer, a man of action: "You are real. A real man of flesh and bone. I am really afraid of you." [18] Hoederer confers a meaning on things. At his worktable he makes coffee in his own coffeepot:

> It seems real when he touches it. Everything he touches seems real. He pours coffee into the cups; I drink, I watch him drink, and I feel that the real taste of warm coffee is in his mouth.[19]

Such is the privilege of the man who has made a choice and assumed a responsibility; the world in all its fullness again takes shape around him. In exchange for his commitment he receives the town of Argos as a gift after he has made his decision. And in the parallel play by Giraudoux, Egisthe received the same gift in exchange for the responsibility which he had assumed: "This morning I received forever my town as a mother receives her child." [20]

C. COMMITMENT AND SITUATION

But what will make us decide to choose, to take the decisive step? Mathieu's misfortune is that he finds no *reason* to commit his freedom to a definite project. To make a blind commitment for the sole purpose of having a goal is to embrace a system of faith and action repugnant to consciousness.

It would seem that before the war Sartre had not yet discovered the reason that would justify the commitment of freedom. But in 1945 he believes that he has found it: *human solidarity.*

To be sure, it could be objected that in theory *we are not obliged to recognize it* (Roquentin did not). If it is but a value, it is not absolute. There can always be men who pretend to dissociate themselves and to become disinterested; they can be called immoral but can not be repressed.

That is why *Sartre presents solidarity not as a value but as a fact.* He does not say that we *ought* to be solidarity but that we *are.* The whole series of events from 1939 to 1944 illustrates his point: Both those who refrained from acting and those who acted were responsible for the misfortunes suffered during the occupation—because they had failed to put a stop sooner to the rise of fascism, because they had not helped to avoid losing the campaign of 1940, because they were not resisting the occupying forces. Whatever man does, and even if he does nothing, he influences collective events, and it is indeed strange that he has not felt their consequences:

> We are convinced . . . that involvement *can not* be avoided. Even if we were as mute and still as stones, our very passivity would be an action.[21]

Man is linked to the destiny of his age, and by his very existence he plays a role. His individual acts have a repercussion on all others, and if he avoids acting, his failure to act will also have a repercussion on all others. Mathieu will discover the interdependence of acts in defeat, following the debacle of June, 1940, when he is overcome by a feeling of powerlessness and anger; he wanted to withdraw from society, politics, the world, but such a withdrawal was impossible.

> God, I wanted to have nothing to do with the war, with defeat; how was I tricked into becoming involved? He felt rising up inside him the anger of a trapped animal; raising his head, he saw the same anger burning in their eyes. He heard them shouting to the heavens in unison: "We have nothing to do with these events! We are innocent!" His ardor cooled: innocence was indeed flooding the morning sky; you could touch it on the blades of grass. But it was lying: Truth was the intangible and common mistake—*our* mistake.[22]

Thus man is no longer an isolated individual. He is involved in spite of himself in the collective life on which he depends and which depends on him. It might seem that the very *responsibility* which was at the outset the basis of Sartre's moral philosophy ceases here to be a moral value, a responsibility freely assumed, inasmuch as it is *automatic*, inevitable, *imposed by his situation.*

And it is true that for Sartre moral values can not be grounded on a responsibility assumed through factual necessity. What, then, is a moral act? It consists of *becoming aware* of this responsibility and of acting accordingly. To be sure, the responsibility is inherent in every man, but only implicitly. It is possible for a man to want to ignore it and for him to hide it from himself. In that case, it will not cease to be valid for him, but he will not acknowledge its validity and will not act correctly as he otherwise might. It is not so much human solidarity that constitutes a value, therefore, since it exists even when denied, but it is rather the courage to look directly at *the interdependence of human destinies* and to agree to play a role in the fray.

* * *

Even as he dissociates himself from world events and chooses not to see that he is thereby precipitating the storm that is gathering overhead, Mathieu is responsible. Only he will not acknowledge it, and *Roads to Freedom* records the stages in his recognition of his responsibility.

The Reprieve, the second volume of the trilogy, appeared in 1945 at the same time as *The Age of*

Reason. In it he tries to bring into focus the inter-dependence of human destinies, which makes it possible for individual freedom, at first empty and without substance, to come into play. This new novel, which includes all the characters in the first volume, records the events which happen two months later, during the week preceding the capitulation in Munich. But here the technique is different; no longer does he try to show, as in the *Age of Reason,* that Mathieu, too hesitant in making a commitment, fails to find nourishment for his freedom. He tries on the contrary to answer Mathieu, to prove to him that his life depends not only on him and his freedom but on the *Situation* in which he finds himself; here Mathieu, mobilized, can not avoid being aware of the situation, the existence of war.

That is why *The Reprieve* is a vast tragic symphony spanning one tense week in which the destiny of the world was shaped by numbers of individuals. For Daladier, Chamberlain, and Hitler were not alone responsible; all those who waited, all those who acted are also responsible and also involved. The impending war, the collective destiny of nations, and the individual destinies of all were not only in the Berchtesgaden discussions but also in the con-sciousness, the action, and the responsibility of each individual—in the Sudetenland Czech besieged in his house by Henlein's partisans, in the provincial pharmacist who has Fascicle 2 and is getting ready to depart. A collective phenomenon like war is not an entity; it is the juxtaposition of the consciousness and responsibilities of millions of individuals.

The Reprieve shows how the world situation imposes itself on each individual consciousness. Each man continues still to live his own life, but constantly before him is the all-important question of war. To express the multiple presence of an event that concerns everyone, the book is written in a distinctive way: the same sentence may begin with a description of an individual in Algiers and suddenly, without warning to the reader, shift to someone else in Paris. Sartre shows Chamberlain opening his mouth; then in the next line, to stress the simultaneity of events, he gives instead of Chamberlain's words the thoughts of a man a hundred miles away. The war, that is the question that concerns and transcends each man, is propounded to everyone, and Sartre uses juxtaposition in space to drive home the point:

> At one instant Mathieu was eating, Marcelle was eating, Daniel was eating, Boris was eating, they had instantaneous souls filled to overflowing with clammy little desires; at one instant it would come barded with steel, feared by Pierre, accepted by Boris, desired by Daniel— the great war of the Upright, the foolish war of the whites. At one instant: it burst out in the room in Milan, it escaped through every window, it spilled over with a roar into the Jaegerschmidts, it stalked the ramparts of Marrakech, it enraged the sea, it tore down the buildings along the Rue Royal, it filled Maurice's nostrils with its smell of young bitches and soured milk; in the fields, in the stables, in the back yards of farms, it *did not exist,* it shuttled from pier to pier in the paneled rooms of the Hôtel Dreesen. The old man[23] mopped

his brow and said in a dull voice, "Well, if you like, we shall discuss one by one the articles in your memorandum." [24]

Thus war is decided by no one in particular but *it involves* everybody. Mathieu is free, but he is involved in the war: individual freedom, paltry and unsettled, *is directly affected by external matters.* This composite picture shows that the individual, though free, is the target of everything that happens in the world and depends on the very events that take place instantaneously: men discover their interdependence when throughout the world they wait for the result of Chamberlain's and Hitler's discussions:

Friday, 23 September, 4:30 p.m. in Berlin, 3:30 in London. The Hotel was languishing on the hill, deserted and solemn, an old man inside. In Angoulême, Marseille, Gand, Dover, they were thinking: "What is he doing? It's past 3, why doesn't he come down?" He was sitting in the drawing room with the blinds drawn; his eyes were staring from beneath his heavy brows and his mouth was slightly open, as if he were recalling some distant something from the remote past. He was no longer reading, and the mottled old hand that held the sheaf of papers had dropped to his knees. He turned to Horace Wilson and asked, "What time is it?" and Horace Wilson said, "Four-thirty, almost." The old man lifted his huge eyes, emitted a slight chuckle, and said, "It's warm." A russet warmth, crepitating and spangled, had settled over Europe; people had warmth on their hands, in the depth of their eyes, in their windpipes; they waited, overcome by warmth, dust, and anguish.[25]

Thus the week in Munich seems to provide a corrective for the total freedom given to man: war is forced upon him. For man is free, but only *in a particular situation.*

That notion will allow Sartre to develop further his theory of freedom. To be sure, each man is always free, but he is not confronted, as Mathieu in *The Age of Reason* and Roquentin in *Nausea* believed, by the emptiness and void of indecision. There is *a definite situation,* which is here the threat of war. Obviously the individual retains a certain freedom which is in a sense complete: he can answer the call to arms, he can cross over into Switzerland, or he can commit suicide. He is free, but *free with respect to an ineluctable question.*

* * *

In point of fact, it could be objected that Sartre's absolute affirmation of freedom as formulated up to this point is untenable since complete freedom is impossible: the poor man is not free to undertake a cruise to Japan, and the prisoner in his cell is not free to order lobster thermidor. If on the one hand it seems that each individual is free always to choose one of several solutions, on the other hand it seems that he is limited by his heredity, his birth, his social class, his nation. All these factors constitute his situation, and *it is only in this situation and with respect to it that he is free.* To say that a poor man is free does not mean that he can indulge in all the follies of a rich man but that, once he realizes that he is poor, he is free to accept his poverty or to complain or to try to become rich. A shy person is free to keep silent or to force himself to speak. A coward is free to flee from danger or to force himself to confront it directly. Mathieu can take the war seriously or lightly, he is then free, but only by virtue of the fact that he accepts his situation—war.

We must therefore recognize our situation before we can be truly free; and *it is then with respect to our situation that we are free to transform it or not.*

> We must regard this freedom neither as a metaphysical power inherent in human nature, nor as license to do as we please, nor as some unidentified inner refuge which we would have even in bondage. We do not do as we please, yet we are responsible for what we are: that is the brute fact.[26]

The importance of this new idea to Sartre's philosophy is obvious. Defined in isolation, *freedom could not justifiably be committed.* But if freedom exists *only with respect to concrete circumstances,* then it affords *concrete solutions.* It follows that *we must not hide from ourselves our situation,* like those who do not wish to see war and the necessity of acting and who, because they reject freedom, find no real food for their freedom of choice.

It must here be noted that for Sartre every moral concept has a double meaning: man is free from the outset because he gives to things a signification and consequently by nature since on him depends the meaning of the world. But if he refuses to make use of his freedom, if he is satisfied with predetermined meanings for things, if he lets himself be duped by life's comedies and plays a role instead of living in the true sense of the word, he alienates his freedom. There is therefore a second way of being freedom, and that is to be *completely* free by avoiding routine. Likewise, man is responsible but can flee from his responsibility; he becomes fully conscious of his responsibility only if he takes risks and deliberately assumes the consequences of his acts. Finally, everyone is totally involved with everyone else since failure to act influences the progress of the world and since the progress of the world will eventually involve everyone, but this theoretical solidarity is different from conscious solidarity. Sartre in his description of man obviously records certain facts: freedom, responsibility, solidarity. But these facts become *values* only if we confront them directly, and *it is by confronting them that we make values of them*. Thus we find here once again the hallmark of his philosophical point of departure, the primacy of consciousness and lucidity.

* * *

The technique employed by Sartre in *The Reprieve* emphasized the solidarity of human destinies rather than Mathieu's awareness. We find again Mathieu in *Troubled Sleep,* the third volume of *Roads to Freedom,* among a crowd of routed soldiers abandoned by their officers and waiting almost with a sense of relief for the Germans to take them prisoners. A wave of humiliation engulfs Mathieu and he wants to fight back. He has discovered that freedom has value only to the extent that it is exercised, that it entails a commitment and a responsibility as well as a precise action in a given situation; against this, in *The Age of Reason* freedom was to him nothing more than an excuse for caution. He tries to make contact once again with the concrete reality of action and exaction which he had always avoided. Morose and ashamed as a result of the debacle, he wants to *affirm* himself. We see him first write his name on a tree, as if afraid that no trace of this overly cautious man will remain; when the armistice is announced, he gives vent to his powerless rage by picking a quarrel with the bravest of his comrades, just as the latter, Pinette, tries to compensate for the humiliation of being defeated through his feminine conquests. A sickening spree staged by idle soldiers resigned to the captivity that awaits them provokes anew in Mathieu the need for trying to discover solidarity, even in shame, by joining them and drinking with them against his wishes. But such half measures are to no avail: he sees clearly that to make his way into the real world he must first have the courage to act, to make use of his freedom, to become conscious of the real meaning of solidarity, to throw on the scale the weight of his responsibility. The man who was afraid to act must "lose himself in an unknown act as in a forest. An act. An act of commitment that is never wholly comprehensible." [27] Finally a detachment of troops arrives, charged with the suicide mission of delaying the German army. While his comrades hide in the cave, Mathieu takes a rifle and with the troops climbs the village belfry.

He has understood that wholly to assume the human condition is to introduce changes and modifications in the meaning of the world: to act.

High up in the belfry, firing with a rifle against the cannons and tanks of the German army, he is making a gesture which is probably futile but which epitomizes his renunciation of all the effeminate precautions of his life and his affirmation of the fact that to live is to incur risks:

> He drew near the parapet and stood there firing. It was a colossal act of revenge; each shot avenged a previous misgiving. One for Lola whom I was afraid to rob, one for Marcelle whom I should have ditched, one for Odette whom I should have seduced. This one for the books that I dared not write, this for the trips I never took, this for everybody I ever wanted to hate and tried to understand.[28]

Thus he atones for all his past shortcomings and goes down in an orgy of affirmation:

> He fired, and the commandments flew through the air—Thou shalt love thy neighbor as thyself—bang! right in that mug—Thou shalt not kill—bang! right in that bastard's face. He fired on Man, on Virtue, on Freedom, on the World: Freedom is terror. A fire raged in the town hall, raged in his head.[29]

There is still something slightly childish in Mathieu's particular act of assumption: he wants not so much to save occupied France as to prove to himself that until now he has been wrong, that if man is destined to bring significations into the world, he must not apply the word lucidity to a cult of the self but to a full knowledge of the world and a bold decision to mold it as he sees fit. Even his sacrifice is theoretical, as befits his character. Militant Brunet, his chronological successor in the Trilogy, does not define Sartre's concept of concrete commitment; the only published extracts from *The Last Chance* depict a disoriented character.

D. MORAL VALUES

GOOD AND EVIL

But human freedom and the very concept of man have acquired a new meaning. Man who is nothing, so close to nothingness, attached to things, yet the sole instrument for bringing significations into the world, is a "project." His worth derives not from his looking on his existence as established and confirmed but rather from his conferring on it a new signification by assuming an irrevocable responsibility.

False was the freedom in *The Age of Reason,* which consisted of contemplating the world with detachment. Only in action does freedom acquire its real meaning for Mathieu. In the same way Oreste, placed in the same situation in *The Flies,* can say:

"*My* deed is done, Electre. . . . I'll carry it on my shoulders as a ferryman carries passengers;

I'll deposit it on the other side and give an accounting of it. And the heavier it is to carry, the happier I'll be, for it is my freedom. Yesterday I was still walking aimlessly on the earth, and thousands of roads eluded my steps, for they belonged to others. . . . Today, there is but one road, and God alone knows where it leads: but it is my own.''[30]

Man's sole grandeur is defined by his personal responsibility for an individual choice effected in the face of a situation presented from without:

Thus freedom is discovered only in action and is intimately fused with it. . . . It is not an innate virtue that gives us license to break away from the most compelling situation. . . . It is rather the power to commit ourselves to the task at hand and to construct a future.[31]

Flung into a world he did not desire, born against his will, unjustified in a situation he did not choose, man is for Sartre sheer creation, summed up *in the possibility of making decisions with respect to a given situation*: "A life is constituted by the future as bodies are constituted by the void." [32]

It is clear, then, that Sartre rejects the *existence* of predetermined values and that he posits *values* to be created. The world offers a situation which seems to limit our freedom and men respond through a project. "The world in which they live is never defined except by reference to the future that they project before them." [33] And what seems immoral to Sartre is to refuse perpetual creation, to fall back upon static values of the past.

Sartre confers a dynamic meaning on the word value, takes issue with the notion of civilization as a fixed accumulation, and thus advances rigorously and imperatively the moral tendency characteristic of most of his predecessors and contemporaries. Whatever already exists, he says, must be transcended: "The revolutionist is such because he *transcends* his situation."[34] His moral philosophy rests on perpetual creation, for the world offers situations that are forever new. There is no wisdom of the ages to serve as a guide, no past experience to compromise the future, no universal value. For Sartre the existentialist condemns universals as such, holding that there are no congealed essences to be revered but only a perpetually renewed existence to be ceaselessly justified anew. He represents a generation which remains aloof from the idea of tradition in order to renew rather than to observe civilization and, in Bernanos' words, in order to make life an adventure rather than an established order.

Man in Sartre's view is never bound by previous obligations, never limited by prefigurations or models; he is forever emerging, unchecked by the past. He is therefore totally free since his acquisitions never commit his future. "Man is not the sum of what he has but the totality of what he still lacks, of what he might have."[35] Freedom with respect to our acquisitions and our past does not entail immorality, for to the extent that he frees us from the past, Sartre impresses upon us the urgency of our *responsibility for the future*. Since man is the totality not of his acquisitions but of his projects, he is responsible for these projects, and especially so since he has behind him in the past no excuse and no

115

motivation. We have to consider what *is* only as it relates to what we shall do. What *is* is already dead, only what *is to be* is living; that is why in his ontology man, who is living, *is* not.

Departing from the traditional idea of the continuum of civilization, Sartre does not think that one can be bound *at the same time* by the *past* and by the *future*. The affirmation of this incompatibility is at the heart of his moral philosophy. He fears that when too much value is attributed to the past, the future is corrupted and compromised.

* * *

It follows that for Sartre Good and Evil are variable realities *relative to each particular situation and that they are not reducible in advance to a code.* He maintains that moral conduct is linked not to a set of immutable precepts but to a truly moral life which is perpetual creation. Here we rediscover the opposition between the two aspects of morality which Bergson had emphasized in a slightly different way; and it is obvious that by seeing it only as creation and never as capitalization he exposes himself to the charge of immorality on the part of those who believe that Good and Evil constitute organic systems of fixed values.

The notion of the existence of Good and Evil, absolute and invariable, is attacked by Sartre in *Lucifer and the Lord.* Goetz, the hero of the work, is fettered by his false belief until he manages to rid himself of it. The action takes place during the final, uncertain years of the Middle Ages; this period, which seems to have a strong grip on our contemporary dramatists, was marked by the ebullition of the Reformation, by peasant revolts, and by the spreading of heresies. Goetz, a bastard and the leader of a band in the service of the bishops and barons engaged in the postfeudal German quarrel, is only too willing to betray his masters. Humiliated by his dubious birth, he works only Evil, joyfully and proudly. Obviously Goetz here believes along with Sartre that Evil is an absolute, for it is postulated as such. One evening when treason and baseness are rife in his camp the leader of the mercenary *reiters* is asked by the girl accompanying him, "Why do Evil?"

> *Goetz.*—Because Good has already been done.
> *Catherine.*—Who did it?
> *Goetz.*—God the Father. I make up things.[36]

But Goetz is challenged by a priest who, aware of having committed an infamous act, in his despair goes so far as to proclaim the absolute reign of Evil:

> *Goetz.*—Then everybody does Evil?
> *Heinrich.*—Everybody.
> *Goetz.*—And nobody has ever done Good?
> *Heinrich.*—Nobody.
> *Goetz.*—Perfect. (*He goes back into his tent.*)
> I'll bet I can.[37]

The artifice that motivates the play is easily discerned: the notion of a contrast between Good and Evil. Sartre wants to show the falsity of this blanket notion, which never really existed other than as a certain element in nineteenth-century bourgeois pharisaism. It makes possible Goetz's wager, which

117

is but a challenge: to be wholly and exclusively Good.

But to realize his project Goetz embraces a *theoretical Good* instead of *defining Good according to circumstances.* For that reason he fails, suffers total degradation, and brings to ruin and devastation the land to which he wanted to bring happiness. He then discovers that Good is not a rigid theoretical notion but a concrete reality.

Sartre lays on religion the blame for propounding the rigid theoretical notion of an immutable Good that reveals itself as a force of destruction. He sees in it a rigid doctrine which provides a blanket definition of Good, and he discovers in it the sign of the Law rather than the sign of Grace. It is therefore Religion, and with it God, that he makes responsible for the mistake. At the end of the play Goetz discovers that "no one can decide for others what is good for them." [38] For Sartre sees in Christianity a doctrine *that imposes a ready-made notion of goodness,* a sort of Pharisaism, and he is wholly sincere in his belief even though he may have failed to consider all the facts. All that Goetz can do is to rid himself of his illusion by opposing to the law of God the life of men; "What I love is this flesh and this life. Only on earth and against God is it possible to love." [39] Abandoning the theory of Good and Evil that has led him astray, he proclaims: "I want to be a man among men." [40] In *The Flies,* too, God in the form of Jupiter is presented as a sort of tyrant who imposes on men a petrified notion of Good: "For the world is good; *I* created it according to my own will and I am Good." [41] Sartre usually depicts

118

a God infatuated with his own person and his creation:

> Good is inside of you, outside of you: it cuts through you like a scythe, it crushes you down like a mountain, it sweeps you up and spins you around like the sea.[42]

We have frequently compared Sartre with Bernanos, but here their similarity ends. Obviously, a God who brandishes his thunderbolts incites man to revolt. Oreste cries out: "What do I care about Jupiter? Justice is the work of men, and I don't need God to teach me that." [43] In the same vein Goetz exclaims: "There was only me: I alone was responsible for Evil; by myself I invented Good." [44] Man is free: "Once freedom has exploded in a human soul, the Gods are powerless." [45] In short, Sartre again takes up the classic argument of the philosophical incompatibility of divine freedom and human freedom.

It is curious to note that the theme of *Lucifer and the Lord* had already been dealt with in the seventeenth century, and this moreover with the same predilection for abusive and didactic oversimplifications, by the Spanish dramatist Tirso de Molina. And his play *El condenado por desconfiado,* which seems not to have been condemned as heretical, is quite similar to Sartre's play. In Tirso's play a hermit and a robber who both live in the mountains happen to meet. Like Goetz, the hermit also believes that there is a set notion of Good: he therefore lives in solitude, fasts, and practices mortification. He does it, however, not for the love of God, but because he is afraid of being damned, precisely because he rejects loving God and living and instead allows

119

a theoretical and empty notion of Good to come between him and God. His neighbor the pillager, quite similar to the first Goetz who does evil (as a matter of fact Goetz in Sartre's work plays successively the two roles that Tirso de Molina attributes to the bandit and to the hermit), though he does not lead an exemplary existence, retains in spite of his mistakes a love for God and Faith in his salvation. Disheartened by this contradiction, the hermit goes so far as to become a bandit in order to capture the robber, tie him to a tree, and ask him under threat of immediate death whether he is sure of his salvation. Finally, the hermit is damned because he fears being damned and because he has substituted for God a theory of Good, whereas the robber is saved. Thus Tirso de Molina rejects in the name of theological vulgarization the petrified notion of Good which Sartre attributes to Christianity.

* * *

Sartre objects to the theoretical nature assumed at times by the notion of Good and Evil. In short, he advocates the concrete in contrast to the abstract, the creative in contrast to the conventional. A moral act should reflect creative choice and not blind obedience. That is why he likes to place his characters in extreme situations in which they are up against a solid wall, so to speak, and ordinary rules are useless. The heroes in *The Victors* are in such a situation: trapped, they have been locked in an attic and are expecting to be tortured. In this situation man is naked in the face of his own truth. "I knew," says one of the Resistance fighters, "that one day I would be up against a solid wall, helpless." [46] They must be true to themselves, must not concoct false problems and false questions. It is no other than Canoris who gives to a companion the advice that Tirso de Molina's play might offer to Goetz:

> You worry too much about yourself, Henry; you want to save your own life[47] . . . Nonsense! You have to work; that way you'll save yourself in the bargain.[48]

Sartre shows a predilection for extraordinary situations in which moral values are determined outside the bounds of ordinary rules: all are persuaded that the youngest and the weakest of them will break down under torture, as he himself admits, and will inevitably bring about the death of their leader. Have they the right to kill him before he breaks down since all of them are already condemned men anyway?

And without a doubt the same predilection for extreme situations in which a man fully realizes one possible predicament caused Sartre to manifest an interest in the writer Jean Genêt, who has experienced to the fullest certain atrocious situations. "Bad" in every sense of the word, Genêt appeals to Sartre as a man who realizes and assumes his position: "I have decided to be what my crime has made me." [49] It is in this sense that he lives out an exceptional adventure on the fringe of society—an adventure which Sartre, in 575 pages, does not hesitate to compare with those of Mallarmé: "Genêt, when he writes, again takes up Igitur's adventure." [50]

* * *

To frame the moral problem outside the context in which the anodyne of convention is effective and to bring man face to face with total, inexorable responsibility, such is the aim of most of the plays and scenarios produced by Sartre between 1945 and 1951. Man's responsibility also entails unlimited freedom to act, to transform the world, to make commitments. Man's possibilities are underscored by the "dead" in *No Exit* and in *The Chips are Down*, for they suffer most from no longer being able to change in any way their lives or the world:

> "You always die too early, or too late. And still life is there, terminated; it's all set down, ready to add up. You are your life and that's it." [51]

And in *The Chips Are Down*, Eve, a disembodied spirit who sees the living but lacks the power to influence their lives, says on noticing in a crowd a little girl about to be robbed of her purse "How horrible it is not to be able to do anything." [52]

For to do something is to modify once more the meaning of our existence and the meaning of the world and thereby to assume the value of human life.

NOTES

Chapter IV

1. *Les Mouches, Théâtre*, pp. 23-24.
2. *Théâtre*, p. 60.
3. *Ibid.*, p. 26.
4. *Théâtre*, p. 62.

5. Cf. Giraudoux, *Combat avec l'ange*, p. 62: "The gods that men have created meet every human requirement. That is indeed cause for suspicion."

6. *Théâtre*, p. 63.

7. *Ibid.*, p. 101.

8. *L'Age de raison*, p. 9.

9. *L'Age de raison*, p. 53.

10. *Ibid.*, p. 57.

11. *L'Age de raison*, p. 53.

12. *Ibid.*, p. 195.

13. *La Nausée*, p. 202.

14. *Les Mouches, Théâtre*, p. 24.

15. *L'Age de raison*, p. 127.

16. *La Mort dans l'âme*, p. 213.

17. *Le Sursis*, p. 219.

18. *Les Mains sales*, p. 240.

19. *Les Mains sales*, p. 132.

20. Giraudoux, *Electre*, p. 178.

21. *Situations* II, p. 13.

22. *La Mort dans l'âme*, p. 50.

23. Chamberlain, to Hitler.

24. *Le Sursis*, p. 59.

25. *Le Sursis*, p. 7.

26. *Situations* II, pp. 26-27.

27. *La Mort dans l'âme*, p. 77.

28. *La Mort dans l'âme*, p. 193.

29. *Ibid.*

30. *Théâtre*, p. 84.

31. *Situations* III, pp. 205-206.

32. *L'Age de raison*, p. 216.

33. *Situations* II, p. 312.

34. *Situations* III, p. 179.

35. *Situations* I, p. 80.

36. *Le Diable et le Bon Dieu*, p. 89.

37. *Ibid.*, p. 149.

38. *Le Diable et le Bon Dieu*, p. 159.

39. *Ibid.*, p. 238.

40. *Ibid.*, p. 275.

41. *Théâtre*, p. 98.

42. *Ibid.*, p. 99.

43. *Ibid.*, p. 80.

44. *Le Diable et le Bon Dieu*, p. 267.
45. *Théâtre*, p. 79.
46. *Théâtre*, p. 183.
47. In the sense "save the meaning of your life" and not "preserve your existence" or "avoid death."
48. *Théâtre*, p. 246.
49. *Saint-Genêt, comédien et martyr*, p. 64.
50. *Ibid.*, p. 529.
51. *Théâtre*, p. 160.
52. *Ibid.*, p. 53.

V. FROM WRITER TO POLITICAL ANALYST

A. ART AND ACTUALITY

Sartre's controversial ideas have aroused opposition from many quarters and the scenes which he has elected to depict in his novels have proven shocking, yet his literary talent has never been questioned. Though it has often been labeled "cleverness," it shows up unmistakably in the dramatic construction of his theatrical works as well as in the structuring of his philosophical ideas. More than a craftsman, Sartre is an artist.

His language, whether descriptive or analytical, is *engaging,* and this for the reason that he encloses himself in the consciousness of one of his characters.[1] His statements thereby take on a certain *intimacy* and his *style* of writing is identified with the style of thinking of each of his characters. Everything is seen through the individualized consciousness of Roquentin, or Mathieu Delarue, or Daniel Sereno, and we become aware even of their sour unsavory smell. This is the salient characteristic of Sartre's novels; what in another writer would be objective narration is colored by the *nature of the human consciousness which is living out the event.* We are not merely present during the events experienced by

Mathieu; we experience the peculiar dryness in his throat, the peculiar mustiness in the depth of his soul. To the reality seen through the eyes of the man chosen as the hero is added the affective halo characteristic of the living subject. Mathieu's visceral and anesthetic reactions to street scenes are conveyed directly to us:

> He felt mellow and expansive and was bothered by the fear of fainting. Still there was in him a sort of stubborn satisfaction. . . .[2]

Thus Sartre's fictional world is not laid out for us with objective detachment but is rather imposed on us along with a certain aftertaste determined by an individual consciousness and a certain succession of moods corresponding to the reality experienced by us, and his style of writing, by forcing us to follow the movement of the book and to be as familiar with the consciousness of the protagonist as with our own, *fascinates us through its subjective intimacy.*

Marcel Proust had in a sense attempted much the same thing by linking the lived reality to the subjective taste of the sponge-cake in order to make the reader experience the event. But whereas Proust preserved a certain analytical detachment and sought somewhat esthetically to reconstruct the past through inimitable impressions, Sartre employs total realism and follows *in the present* the movement and mood of a consciousness. And it is probably on account of this, rather than on account of his daring descriptions and lewd scenes, that the reader's initial reaction is one of shame and at times disgust.

But to depict such familiarity Sartre must be

steeped in the minutiae of human intimacy, composed of lost thoughts, abortive movements, and fleeting hesitations and impressions. That is why his narrative, without losing any of its density, may take in the most banal facts which constitute the usual dull life of consciousness and which Jules Romains alone had previously managed to depict.

The exterior world, neglected at first by Sartre, takes on new life as it is subdued by consciousness and gives rise to the beautiful and imposing images of *Roads to Freedom*:

> The night was gentle and unsullied, the flesh so often rent by darkness had scabbed over. A virgin, all-embracing night, a night without men, a beautiful bloodstone without blemishes. Regretfully [Daniel] closed the Venetian blinds and turned on the switch; the room leaped from the shadows and things regained their identity.[3]

Mathieu roaming vainly through the deserted summer streets in Paris confers on the world his meaning and imbues it with harshness:

> In the distance a little girl was skipping a rope; it rose above her head like a giant arch and lashed the dirt under her feet. One summer afternoon the light had settled on the street and on the housetops, uniform, rigid, and cold like an eternal truth.[4]

Appearances obey the fluctuations of consciousness: Mathieu in Juan-les-Pins reflects on the imminent war. Coming out of his reverie, he again becomes aware of the beach and his surroundings:

> Suddenly the sea was again there, and the whispering of the waves and the Chinese shadows running over the waves and the caress of the sun probing the sea, and the green agaves and the green needles carpeted the ground and the pointillist shadow of the tall pines and the uniform white heat and the smell of resin, all the heaviness of a September morning in Juan-les-Pins.[5]

Consciousness, *always the center of everything*, finds an order and a meaning in things, and Sartre favors particularly twilight images conducive to a critical examination of the earth's surface: at dawn in 1938 Mathieu, called into active service and ready to take the train, finds that a seemingly empty day opens the perspective of an unknown future—war:

> There it was, this full, round day, about to fade away calmly; suddenly it stretched out and crashed like an arrow into the heart of night; it fled into the darkness, into the smoke, into the deserted fields, across the clatter of axle-trees and conveyances and slipped inside as if in a toboggan; it did not stop until it reached the end of night, at the Lyon station in Paris.[6]

And at twilight in June, 1940, on the French plains lying in wait for the German occupation:

> The earth and fields reverted suddenly to their primeval uselessness; in the midst of fields

128

which they could neither cultivate nor defend, men became gratuitous. Everything seemed new and yet the evening was decked out in the dark ribbon of on-coming night.[7]

But the life of things is that of consciousness, the sole creator of significations, which casts on them the image of its situation or project. Sartre never interrogates things themselves and he disparages any attempt to coax from words and from reality irrational significations:

> Nothing is less auspicious than the literary exercise called, I believe, poetic prose, which consists of using for the sake of the obscure harmonies that flow from them vague words rather than precise words.[8]

He therefore rejects the heritage of Rimbaud and the surrealists:

> We are no longer concerned with igniting the underbrush of language, with mating "words that strike fire" and attaining the absolute through the combustion of the dictionary.[9]

What Is Literature? (1947) rejects poetic, artistic, and metaphysical literature in favor of prose designed to influence men morally, socially, and politically. Its aim is to "communicate with other men by using unpretentiously the resources at their disposal." [10]

* * *

His position is a logical consequence of his concept of commitment, that is, of the affirmation of *responsibility* which, *though automatic and inescapable, must still be recognized if it is to be most fruitful.* Sartre deems it impossible for anyone, including writers, to be disinterested in the world of affairs since sooner or later it will influence his own life. Moreover, he had already stated that to live is actually to take part in transforming the world:

> It is not in some esoteric haunt that we discover ourselves, it is on the highway, in town, in the middle of the crowd, as a thing among things, a man among men.[11]

Man is not a self-contained reality but a project—a possibility of giving meaning to the world. He can be summed up as a choice made in, concerning, and against the world:

> And for this choice he alone is responsible. He is not free not to choose: he is committed, he must take a stand, abstention is choice.[12]

We must therefore come to grips with our age, for it is *ours* and we are not allowed to take refuge in eternity. We must *take sides*: "For us, to write is to commit ourselves, for we must live before we can die." [13] It might be objected that art is not compelled to reflect actuality. Sartre's answer is that "we admire the *art* of *Provinciales* . . . and yet they dealt with contemporary issues." [14]

Beauty and art are in Sartre's opinion pretexts for failing to confront directly the issues of the age.

While not denying them outright, he relegates them to a secondary place: "In prose, esthetic pleasure is pure only if accessory." [15] We ought to write first in order to say something to the living; so much the better if something admirable in our style appeals to our grand-nephew even though he can no longer appreciate the worth of our writings in terms of the contemporary issues with which they dealt. But style must not be cultivated for its own sake; sincerity and responsibility take first place, while style and beauty are accessory.

He holds that mind must not hover over events but be united with them, and here he provides a prop for intellectuals who take offense when deemed "abstract" and "far removed from reality." Of course abstraction is characterized, etymologically at any rate, by withdrawal from reality; but recognition of such a withdrawal has no part in Sartre's definition. Contemporary issues must confer on works of the mind their prime worth:

> It seems that bananas taste best right after they have been plucked from the plant: in the same way the fruits of the mind ought to be for immediate consumption.[16]

B. POLITICAL COMMITMENTS AND THE DIRECTOR OF *LES TEMPS MODERNES*

Until 1946 Sartre had won recognition as a writer both through the interest of the public in his ideas and through his literary talent. The bulk of his writings, ranging from the publication of *Nausea* (1938) to the appearance of *Roads to Freedom* (1946) accounted for the universal renown of Sartre the writer.

Can it be said that since 1946 Sartre has ceased to be a writer? Not exactly, for he has not completely abandoned the so-called literary genres; in addition to *Troubled Sleep* (1949), the third volume of *Roads to Freedom,* he has also written four plays—actually thesis plays. But he has not published another novel. He has even ceased to be a philosopher in the general sense of the word and instead has become a political analyst. He has become the editor of a political journal, *Les Temps Modernes*; he has apparently elected to give direction to a philosophy rather than to create in his own right, to translate his aims through his work in shaping opinion rather than through creative works. Gradually his role as a writer has been supplanted by his role as an intellectual organizer of a political faction. Between the vocation of Gide and that of Mounier—he had been quite familiar with the latter—Sartre has chosen Mounier.

It would be wrong to think that the choice marks the depletion of his energy and that it portends impotence, senescence, a detour, or a blunder. The truth is that Sartre is convinced that the writer has no right to create works which, though convincing, represent but symbolic fictions with respect to reality. His duty is on the contrary to *analyze directly the political reality*, and this entails becoming a journalist, a polemicist, a theoretician and an analyst, and not a purveyor of things imagined, confessions, inner struggles. That is why he speaks the language of the political and social sciences and resorts to their style and their method of analyzing facts sociologically rather than in the intimacy of an individual consciousness. No longer does he evoke a certain pathetic autumn afternoon of 1938 and show its effects on the consciousness of an individual:

> Tons of heat and war weighed down on the sea, on the sand, and there was this shrieking of a mouse that rose to high heaven.[17]

Instead he writes:

> Dialectics forces us to envision a proletariat-subject in history, a substance and guaranty of the proletariat-object in sociology. This immediately implies the dialectical reversal of the terms: the existence of the empirical proletariat, by administering the *proof of the fact*, becomes in turn the guaranty.[18]

Here he is no longer a writer but a political analyst, and one who still has all the earmarks of a scholar and a professor. Once the terms are defined it is possible for us to say that Sartre is no longer a writer and for him to say in turn that the duty of the true writer is to write as he does and on his themes, and that is exactly what he maintains in *What Is Literature?* Here he shows that every man, and especially the writer, is linked solely and inseparably to the larger historical and social context in which he lives:

> The writer is *in situation* in his era: each word has its repercussions. Each silence as well. I hold Flaubert and Goncourt responsible for the repression that followed the Commune because they failed to write a line to prevent it.[19]

He condemns the detachment which artists, thinkers, intellectuals, and ascetics have at times seen fit to practice. He sees in their actions an instance of bad faith which can not endure after the facts are brought to light:

> For a hundred years the writer has dreamed of giving himself over to his art in a state of innocence, beyond Good as well as Evil and, in a sense, before the Fall. It is society that has placed on our shoulders our charges and our duties.[20]

The result is that the writer is neither "Vestale nor Ariel: no matter what he does, he is forever marked, found out, even in the most distant retreat."[21] Once again he makes of commitment not a duty but *a fact*. Duty consists only of drawing out the consequences of the fact:

> Since the writer can in no way practice self-evasion, we would have him fervently embrace his era; it is his only chance: it is made for him and he for it. We regret Balzac's indifference to the happenings of '48, Flaubert's appalling failure to understand the Commune; we are sorry for *them*, for there was something that they missed forever. We would miss nothing in our era; it may not be the best, but it is ours; we have but *this* life to live, right in the middle of *this* war, *this* revolution perhaps.[22]

Furthermore, Sartre's writings give the impression that he feels a certain nostalgia for the life of a combatant. It is possible that every man at one time in his life regrets not having become a pilot, a sailor, or a Don Juan. A professor and a member of the middle class—with respect to his objective situation, at any rate—Sartre seemed to dream of the leather-jacketed combatant who participated with others in his group in fraternal and clandestine meetings. This dream appears in *Roads to Freedom* in the person of Brunet, the communist for whom action is always difficult and always mandatory, whose every act has a meaning, and whose life is made radiant by the seriousness of the charge which he has accepted. It appears again in his two scenarios, *The Chips Are Down* and *In the Mesh*.[23] In these two scenarios, what little intrigue there is serves only to contrast combatants with the *motards* in the Regent's militia. Passwords, the front, etc. create an atmosphere that visibly appeals to the author, a middle-class intellectual who longs to find a place in the brotherhood of men but can not. *Dirty Hands*[24] unfolds in the same atmosphere.

It would therefore seem that Sartre's own fictional world is linked to a more intellectual element, and that together they incite him to want literature to be a *real* political force. Early in life he had become aware that he was fated, in spite of his longing for action, to be a man of letters rather than a man of action, and he describes with a trace of bitterness the rigidity of his cloistered life in the Parisian community:

> We are always found together—or most of us, anyway—in certain cafés, at the Pléiade concerts and, on certain purely literary occasions, at the British Embassy. Occasionally one of us, over-

135

come by it all, announces that he is leaving for the country and that we should all come to see him; we assure him that he is doing what is best for him, that no one could possibly write in Paris, and we send him merrily on his way.[25]

He sees about him the closed and familiar circle of the literary world that imprisons him and his reputation:

> After our first book appears, five years is time enough for us to shake the hand of each of our colleagues. Centralization brings us all to Paris; with a little luck, an American who is in a hurry can join us in twenty-four hours.[26]

He has every reason to believe that literature can transform the world and have a direct influence on readers by resorting to vulgarization, and he examines the problem:

> Have recourse to new techniques: they already exist; the Americans have already dignified them by the name "mass media"; they are our best resources for conquering our potential public—the press, radio, films. We must of course not give in to our scruples.[27]

This explains why the esoteric writer has devoted the last several years to sensational film scripts and plays, and often to journalism. "There is a *literary* art in radio and film scripts, in editorial writing, and in reporting." [28] This was true of his reporting in the United States. But in his reports Sartre preserves the main ideas of his system: just as he identifies philosophically the notion of individual responsibility in learned routines, he sees in the United States the conflict between conformity with respect to American mores and individual freedom:

> The system is a great external machine, an implacable machine which might be called the objective mind of the United States and which over there is called Americanism; it is a monstrous complex of myths, values, prescriptions, slogans, figures, and rites. . . . They struggle against it or accept it, they succumb to it or surpass it, they constantly suffer from it or reinvent it, they freely give themselves over to it or struggle furiously to elude it; come what may, it transcends them and stands apart from them, for they are men and it is a thing.[29]

But it was hard to believe that journalism, so long as it was an independent undertaking, could appeal to the writer's sense of responsibility strongly enough to make him turn away from his own fictions and confront "situations." That is why Sartre tried in 1948, with David Rousset and Gérard Rosenthal, to form a new party, the *Rassemblement Démocratique Révolutionnaire*. But it failed to receive the support of the working class as anticipated and was soon dissolved as a result of internal controversies waged by the sensitive intellectuals who had founded it. The party did, however, occasion the publication of a joint work, *Political Discussions (Entretiens sur la Politique)*. As for Sartre's political ideas, they are defined by

> . . . the emergence of a socialist Europe, that is, a number of states with a democratic and col-

lectivist structure; each state, while awaiting something better, would be deprived of a part of its sovereignty for the good of all.[30]

He believes in a European federation which is communal but not communistic, a neutral federation between two blocs but one closer to certain Soviet principles than to the American way of life.

The defeat suffered by those who attempted to spearhead the leftist movement gradually caused Sartre and his journal, always receptive to communistic ideas, to subject contemporary problems to Marxist analysis and to draw up dossiers on crucial issues of the times. For example, *Les Temps Modernes* published special numbers dealing with Viet-Nam (August-September 1953) and the Left (1955).

One might suppose that these analyses of political and social situations mark a complete change from Sartre the writer of 1946. They are nevertheless the result, in a more restricted area, of the same method as that employed in *Being and Nothingness*. From the phenomenological viewpoint, philosophy should analyze structures rather than aim at an arbitrary and ideal reconstruction of the world. As a philosopher in the usual sense of the term, Sartre analyzed the structures of consciousness: for instance, patterns of conduct involving bad faith, the game which consists of seeing ourselves in the eyes of the Other. As a philosopher in a more restricted sense—as a political analyst—Sartre also analyzes structures; here, however, he has in mind social structures.

If there has been a change, it stems from the fact that in 1943 Sartre was still a practitioner of abstract philosophy; he was interested in the relations of consciousness and things, like Descartes or Kant. Today he would probably accuse himself of having been a bourgeois philosopher or a philosopher afflicted with chronic idealism, for today he seems no longer to be interested in the life of consciousness but instead in the objective social world. He has never defined his position today in contrast to that outlined in his earlier works in which he rejected the postulates of materialism, giving first place to consciousness and denying that it can have its origin in the material world. But here as in the psychological analyses in his novels, he has renounced the developments of abstract philosophy and restricted his attention to the analysis of structures—political structures, for the most part, and only rarely structures belonging to the world of art.[31]

In his political writings Sartre goes beyond analysis and *takes sides*. He rejects the attitude often characteristic of the writer faced with crucial issues of the times: a moral conscience which, while it does not shirk responsibility, pretends to judge the events from an ivory tower and with impartiality, to study and censure the different parties instead of espousing the cause championed by one of them. He censures Albert Camus[32] for assuming the role of moralist and superimposes on his own role of analyst that of polemicist. He is far from a literary polemicist, however, and disdains—except in his "Reply to Albert Camus" —style and form; in general, he mistrusts the literary art and prefers to it argumentation.

Only on the stage has Sartre tried to provide a literary and symbolic illustration of his theories—or more exactly a vulgarization of some of his theories. In fact, he tends more and more to write what are obviously thesis plays. In them he tries to breathe life, not into certain characters, but into the ideas they champion. *Dirty Hands* (1948) seems to belong still in some ways to the period of uncertainty concerning the character and employment of man's will to act. But in *Lucifer and the Lord* (1951) Goetz follows in the footsteps of Oreste and rediscovers the necessity of acting; he adds the notion that action must henceforth be determined solely by the historical situation toward which it is directed. *Kean* (1954) seems to return to the period of psychological analyses, presenting here the drama of the actor. *Nekrassov* (1955) is a political satire in the form of a farce. All these plays are the product of a master showman with the ability to obtain coarse but cleverly contrived effects through actions and ideas presented on stage. And though the ideas which he seeks to make clear to his audience are perfectly ordered, the characters are puppets manipulated by the author and his thesis. It is obvious that Sartre has renounced—quite willingly, in all probability—his art of evoking, suggesting, or vivifying the intimacy of a consciousness. That is why his dramatic style has become mechanical and seems at times to parody itself, much like the satirical revues presented near the close of the academic year by college students who try to make a parody of acting and who laugh at their own pomposity. As a patron says to an employee:

> Why, there are people who would agree to do it
> for nothing. And you, you who have the oppor-
> tunity to serve the noblest of causes and be paid
> in the bargain, you dare to ask me for a raise?[33]

It is obvious, moreover, that literary considerations are secondary, that Sartre has recourse to "mass media" mainly to illustrate his theories. *Les Séquestrés d'Altona* (1960) satirizes the bourgeoisie: the first-born son and heir to the industrial fortune of a prominent Hanseatic family, because of his Nazi beliefs, has had to pretend to be dead. For ten years, wearing a German officer's uniform, he has been living in a cloistered room; only his sister, to whom he is linked by an incestuous practice, enters the room. But the problem of succession is posed when the father, a captain of industry, falls victim to cancer. The younger son is incompetent; only his wife, the "sequestered" son's sister-in-law, has strength of character. And, triggered by the crisis, the vast complex of lies erected by this middle-class family explodes, creating dramatic situations and reversals. *Les Séquestrés d'Altona* is highly theatrical—at times even grandiloquent and spurious—but always overpowering. It exploits all the resources of the drama; it makes use of exceptional situations and of stock theatrical devices, such as the monocled former SS officer who refuses to read the newspapers and *wishes* to believe that occupied Germany has been held in bondage, deintrustrialized, defrauded. But its impact is incontestable, and the tragicomedy continues to draw large audiences. Ideologically, it contributes nothing new. It merely denounces the will to lie which, according to Sartre, is characteristic of the bourgeoisie. And at the end of the play the father, an industrial opportunist, and his son, the former Nazi officer, set out together to commit suicide in a sham automobile accident. Here the theatre is for Sartre

141

a means of popularizing successive stages in the development of his thought. Here he is showing quite simply the inner contradictions in the lives of a middle-class family, just as Alexandre Dumas, *fils*, had previously done. But the author's dramatic and literary talent permeates the more restricted, and for him easier, medium that he has chosen.

C. NEO-MARXISM AND
CRITICISM OF DIALECTICAL REASONING

Since 1947 Sartre's major writings have been political essays directly related to the contemporary scene. Whether writing about Indo-China, Algeria, American politics, or the Negro problem, he has never denied that for him the only possible system of analysis and line of conduct in the field of action is the Marxist. But the points of departure of historical materialism are not the same as those of Sartre's original philosophy. Marxism takes as its prime datum the biological and social condition of man, whose consciousness is but a "superstructure."

In *Nausea* and in *Being and Nothingness* Jean-Paul Sartre started as did the ancient "idealists" (though he stated the problem differently) from the interiority of consciousness. Marxism starts from something *external* to consciousness—the biological and social datum of the human collectivity and its class structure. There was therefore a rigid philosophical opposition between the Marxist system and Sartre's. Far from concealing this opposition, Sartre still acknowledges it, even after fifteen years of apprenticeship:

We were *at the same time* convinced that historical materialism provided the only valid interpretation of history, and that existentialism constituted the only concrete approach to reality.[34]

The phrase "at the same time" (the italics are Sartre's) shows the dilemma which he faced for years: convinced that he was right in his analysis of man's situation and that the communists were right in their analysis of history, he was tormented by the fact that the Marxist interpretation of history was grounded on a principle which he could not accept. In the preface to his *Criticism of Dialectical Reasoning* (first published in 1957 as "Question of Method"), he affirms without tergiversation that in its present form Communism has become a sterile, compulsory doctrine, that through neglect even its fountainhead remains obstructed:

> After attracting us as the moon attracts the tide, after transforming all our ideas, after effacing in us the categories of bourgeois thought, Marxism suddenly left us on a plateau; it failed to satisfy our need to understand; it no longer had anything to teach us, for it had stopped.[35]

Are we to believe that Sartre is challenging, rejecting, and attacking historical materialism? No. He continues to believe that it affords the only effective instruments for influencing the course of history. But its truth is practical and empirical; its philosophical bases are not solid:

> Why are we not simply Marxists? Because we look upon the statements made by Engels and

143

by Garaudy as *guiding principles,* as suggestions for action, as statements of problems, and not as *concrete truths.*[36]

In other words, Communism never errs *in the sphere of action,* but Communism as a political system has developed at the expense of the philosophy of communism. Here as well as in the doctrine of action, self-criticism should be given free reign:

> It ought to be allowed to take root and develop as free criticism of itself and at the same time as the development of History and knowledge. That is something that has not yet been done; it has been checked by dogmatism.[37]

In his *Criticism of Dialectical Reasoning* Sartre proposes to enrich the philosophical substrata of dialectical materialism, whose *practical* truth he finds incontestable. Contemporary Marxist theory is nothing more than "empirical anthropology,[38] and what is needed is "a dynamic Marxism which will incorporate the disciplines that still remain outside it."[39] These disciplines can all be reduced to phenomenology, which studies the structures of existence and discovers that the primary datum is not the social one but rather the datum of consciousness. In contrast to Marxism, which has as its starting point cosmic, biological, and social elements, Sartre starts from *human experience,* from consciousness, from the individual—even if the individual is the victim of the social conditions under which he lives:

> We refuse to confuse the alienated (oppressed) man with a thing or his alienation with the phys-

ical laws governing external conditions. *We affirm the specific nature of the human act,* which cuts through the social structure even as it preserves determinism.[40]

Putting it another way, Sartre will not look upon man as the simple resultant of the material, biological, and social conditions in which he finds himself. Man is rather a *project* fashioned in his or their *consciousness* by an individual or a group exposed to certain conditions. This is a restatement of the theory of freedom and responsibility expressed earlier in *Being and Nothingness* and in *The Flies.*

The problem is to reconcile Marxism, which explains the individual in terms of his social conditions, and Sartre's philosophy, which cannot avoid giving first place to *what is actually experienced by the individual.* From Marxism Sartre borrows the notion of the dialectic, that is, the development of a reality through several stages and through several forms, each more complex than the one that preceded. But in his *Criticism of Dialectical Reasoning,* the Marxist dialectic ceases to be a social mechanism and becomes instead something experienced by the individual.

Naturally, the experience is not lived through in solitude. In earlier works Sartre had clearly shown that each individual is free and independent *within a situation;* the individual is influenced by his situation, but he can accept it, modify it, or transcend it. In his *Criticism of Dialectical Reasoning,* he points up this basic fact: Marxism posits the lived, individual experience as the reflex of a social phenomenon; analysis of structures (those of the individual consciousness as well as social structures) reveals that this experience is on the contrary the dynamic, concrete, and —this bears repetition—"lived" aspect of the general and social statistical fact to which Marxism attributes the movement of history.

The problem of reconciliation confronting Sartre is therefore what he calls "totalization," or passing from the individual to the group, from consciousness to history. In this process, are individual experiences and actions "totalized" to yield the collective phenomena studied by Marxism?

> The problem, for us, is one of classification. Given individuals, *who* or *what* is to be totalized? [41]

To resolve the issue, Sartre transports "dialectical movement" from the collectivity to the individual and, in contrast to Marxism, sees in consciousness the source of the collectivity; it is the individual that experiences social realities, reacts, develops dialectically, and creates the social dialectic:

> There would be no trace of even partial totalization if the individual were not *himself* totalizing. *The whole structure of the historical dialectic rests on individual praxis insofar as it is already dialectical.*[42]

Thus the historical movement originates in the individual, not through any magical or statistical operation, but because in themselves individuals, in the normal dialectic of their lives, manifest the need for "totalization" which creates the collective phenomenon.

146

Sartre therefore studies in the individual, from the onset of consciousness, the movement that creates History. The titles of the first two parts of his *Criticism* are revealing. In "From Individual *Praxis* to Inert *Praxis*" he shows that man is by nature committed to the (economic) *praxis* on which Marxism is based. This *praxis* is inert so long as it is not historical action; it becomes historical action in the second part, "From the Group to History." And Volume II of his *Criticism* will carry this evolution to its completion.

That is how Sartre reconciles the lived experience (the basis of his philosophy) and the Marxist movement of History, on the one hand, and on the other, freedom and necessity. For every stage through which the individual creates the social "totalization" that will acquire a historical meaning represents a conflict between the necessity that constrains him and freedom that enables him to resist and "transcend" his "situation":

> Freedom and necessity are one and the same. . . .
> It is an individual construction whose sole agents are individual men carrying out their functions as free activities.[43]

That is also how he recreates Marxism and explains it in terms of human freedoms.

* * *

In 1960 Sartre appears as the creator of a *neo-Marxism,* or as one who would adapt orthodox Marxism to the necessities of not abandoning, in favor of

147

the inexorable social mechanism of History, the lived individual experience, and with it the notions of freedom, responsibility, and independence. His able brief is convincing, even if understandable only to other philosophers; for the simple fact is that it was not written for the public at large.

Jean-Paul Sartre, the philosopher and advocate of *neo-Marxism* in 1960, bears scant resemblance to the author of *Nausea* in 1938. Still, the evolution from one to the other is quite obvious and easily explained. Coming on the heels of the generation that had, independently of the pre-war tradition, focused attention on the total freedom of the individual, Sartre emphasized the emptiness of human freedom, the individual's terror in the face of his freedom.

The only answer to the emptiness of freedom is responsibility. In Bernanos, who is after all one of Sartre's contemporaries, it is a spiritual responsibility. In Malraux, it is man's affirmation of himself as a mortal and eternal being. Sartre had chosen, between *Nausea* and *The Flies,* man's *historical* responsibility, and this led him first to Marxism, then to what is rightly termed neo-Marxism. His theory is developed in a work in which the "militant intellectual" and the philosopher win out over the simple man of letters. His more recent works are less seductive than those produced between 1938 and 1947; they are also less accessible to non-militants. It is possible that Sartre deliberately sacrificed his talent and his success as a writer to his historical mission. For his talent has not vanished: a play like *Les Séquestrés d'Altona,* in which the bourgeoisie is subjected to self-criticism, still attracts middle-class audiences whose average age is past fifty. This is one more proof of his talent.

148

In his *Criticism of Dialectical Reasoning*, he seems to disdain talent and to prefer instead difficult, pedantic analyses which, though they reach but a limited public, are of supreme interest to him. There is an element of nobility in his mission and in his near renunciation of "literature."

* * *

D. CONCLUSIONS

Sartre has manifested an interest in the world about him, has taken a stand on crucial issues, and has tried in *Les Temps Modernes* to mold public opinion. At the same time it would seem that he has renounced creative literature in the usual sense of the word, that is, literature that reveals through a subjective pathos certain fictions or situations. And in his case there has been a transformation rather than evolution or conversion.

His transformation is the logical result not of his artistic development but of problems implicit in his writings from 1938 to 1946. *Roads to Freedom* and *The Flies,* though they are literary works, tend to condemn literature as well as the writer who is satisfied to give expression to his musings, and to favor those who act directly. Mathieu Delarue is a savant, a poet, a man of letters; he analyzes his consciousness. But the book about him is designed to show that he is wrong, that it is wrong to analyze consciousness, that what must be analyzed is the historical situation in which we find the individual that constitutes this consciousness.

That is why, once he became convinced of the prime importance of political action, he had to renounce the type of novel that examines the inner conflict over the meaning of life. He could not start over without repeating himself: he had found, if not the meaning, at least the right employment of life and freedom. He was faithful to his own conclusions when he became a political analyst and a polemicist concerned with actual circumstances, when he became a combatant to the extent that an intellectual can be one. He had shown that responsibility is our only answer to the freedom given us; whether in the context of Mathieu Delarue's quiet, independent life, devoid of action and of horizons, or in the face of a tortured world, Sartre, having recognized the overwhelming influence of history on man, could conceive of this responsibility only as historical and political.

* * *

Even if we rejected Sartre's choice and his present views, even if we wished to consider him apart from them, his stature would not be diminished and he would be revealed as one of the writers of our time who, starting from a discouraging examination of the individual, have had sufficient insight and vigor to give back to the individual, both to subdue him and to save him, the notion of responsibility which—whether on the moral, spiritual, social, political, or other plane—is at the heart of an ever-increasing number of works, both literary and polemical.

All of our literature for the last twenty years (or even longer if we disregard the aftermath of estheticism in the twenties) has stressed the primacy of morals over esthetics and has examined crucial issues; it has become a proving ground for the diverse solutions that man can find for the employment of his life. From this research in morals carried out in defiance of traditions and customs and continued today, along with Sartre, by such writers as Anouilh, Camus, and Graham Greene, there emerges above the debris of inherited values the notion of responsibility: Graham Greene advances the paradox of impenitent criminals who remain Catholics because, even if they know they are damned, their Faith makes them feel *responsible*.[44]

Through a long sequence of philosophical notions Sartre establishes man's responsibility and the necessity of making it bear fruit. Despite the harshness and rigidity of some of his ideas, his basic lesson and that of his contemporaries is that in the face of the moral despair of an age that hurls itself more vertiginously than any other toward cataclysms and chaos, and of the futility of habitual and routine behavior, man must hold fast to one thing: the idea that he alone is responsible and yet must act, the will not to give up when he fails to see the path, and the decision to commit himself at his own risk and peril. This constitutes, when all is said and done, the precious and imperative privilege which nothing can destroy. Man may cease to believe in this or that reassuring notion and the world about him may disintegrate, *but he has in his own hands his salvation and his dignity so long as he maintains that he is responsible.*

Sartre expresses in his rigorous and matter-of-fact way the idea that a dozen of the world's great writers have finally discovered and held up as a beacon to guide a universe maimed by catastrophes and darkened by threats. Thus Sartre's methodical work, apart from all anterior and exterior considerations, culminates in the same moral realm, though not in the same moral system, as Bernanos, Camus, and Greene. It tends to isolate man from the life of the Cosmos, to show his limitations and anxieties, to trim to the quick his possibilities, and to impose on him "a man's responsibilities—the stubborn task of saying yes or no according to the rules, of undertaking without hoping, of persevering without succeeding." [45]

NOTES

Chapter V

1. He even refuses the novelist the right to take a point of view that "hovers" over the consciousness of his characters. See his article "Mauriac et la liberté," *Situations* I.
2. *L'Age de raison*, p. 204.
3. *La Mort dans l'âme*, p. 140.
4. *L'Age de raison*, p. 131.
5. *Le Sursis*, p. 89.
6. *Le Sursis*, p. 70.
7. *La Mort dans l'âme*, p. 137.
8. *Situations* II, p. 305.
9. *Ibid.*, p. 34.
10. *Ibid.*, p. 34.
11. *Situations* I, p. 35.
12. *Ibid.*, II, p. 28.
13. *Ibid.*, p. 83.
14. *Ibid.*, p. 76.
15. *Ibid.*, pp. 75-76.
16. *Situations* II, pp. 122-123.
17. *Le Sursis*, p. 24.

18. "Réponse à Lefort," *Les Temps Modernes* (April, 1953), p. 1602.

19. *Situations* II, p. 13.

20. *Situations* II, p. 260.

21. *Ibid.*, p. 12.

22. *Ibid.*, pp. 12-13.

23. Only the first of these has been filmed (by Jean Delannoy).

24. *Les Mains sales*, p. 210.

25. *Situations* II, p. 205.

26. *Ibid.*, p. 290.

27. *Ibid.*, p. 291.

28. *Situations* II, p. 291.

29. *Situations* III, pp. 126-127.

30. *Situations* II, p. 315.

31. "Les peintures de Giacometti," *Les Temps Modernes* (June, 1954).

32. "Réponse à Albert Camus," *Les Temps Modernes* (August, 1952).

33. "Nekrassov," *Les Temps Modernes* (June-July, 1955), p. 2053.

34. *Critique de la raison dialectique,* p. 24.

35. *Ibid.,* p. 25.

36. *Ibid.,* p. 33.

37. *Ibid.,* p. 120.

38. *Ibid.,* p. 117.

39. *Ibid.,* p. 117.

40. *Ibid.,* p. 63.

41. *Ibid.,* p. 165.

42. *Ibid.,* p. 165. Italics are Sartre's.

43. *Ibid.,* p. 377.

44. See Graham Greene, *Brighton Rock.*

45. *Situations* III, p. 53.

I. WORKS BY SARTRE

A. Philosophy

1936. *L'Imagination* (Presses Universitaires). *Psychology and Imagination* (Philosophical Library, 1948).

1937. *Transcendence of the Ego* (Noonday, 1957).

1939. *Esquisse d'une théorie des émotions* (Hermann). *The Emotions, Outline of a Theory* (Philosophical Library, 1948).

1940. *L'Imaginaire, psychologie phénoménologique de l'imagination* (Gallimard). *Psychology of Imagination* (Rider, 1951).

1943. *L'Etre et le Néant* (Gallimard). *Being and Nothingness* (Philosophical Library, 1956) .

1960. *Critique de la raison dialectique,* I (Gallimard)

B. Fiction

1938. *La Nausée* (Gallimard). *Nausea* (New Directions, 1949).

1939. *Le Mur* (Gallimard). *The Wall and Other Stories* (New Directions, 1948).

1945–49. *Les Chemins de la liberté (Roads to Freedom).* I—*L'Age de raison;* II—*Le Sursis;* III—*La Mort dans l'âme* (Gallimard). Published by Knopf: *Age of Reason* (1947); *The Reprieve* (1947); *Troubled Sleep* (1951).

C. Drama

1943. *Les Mouches* (Gallimard). In *No Exit and The Flies* (Knopf, 1947).

1944.	*Huis-clos* (Gallimard). In *No Exit and The Flies* (Knopf, 1947).
1946.	*Morts sans sépulture* (Gallimard). *The Victors,* in *Three Plays* (Knopf, 1949).
1947.	*Les Jeux sont faits* (Nagel). *The Chips Are Down* (Lear, 1948).
1948.	*Les Mains sales* (Gallimard). *Dirty Hands,* in *Three Plays* (Knopf, 1949).
1949.	*L'Engrenage* (Nagel). *In the Mesh* (Dakers, 1954).
1951.	*Le Diable et le Bon Dieu* (Gallimard). In *The Devil and the Good Lord and Two Other Plays* (Knopf, 1960). Published in England as *Lucifer and the Lord* (Hamilton, 1952).
1954.	*Kean* (Gallimard). *Kean,* in *The Devil and the Good Lord and Two Other Plays* (Knopf, 1960).
1955.	*Nekrassov* (Gallimard).
1960.	*Les Séquestrés d'Altona* (Gallimard).

D. Essays on Literature and Politics

1946.	*Descartes* (Trait). Introduction and selected texts.
1947.	*L'Existentialisme est un humanisme* (Nagel). *Existentialism* (Philosophical Library, 1947).
1947.	*Situations* I (Gallimard). Selections in *Literary and Philosophical Essays* (Philosophical Library, 1957).
1947.	*Baudelaire* (Gallimard). *Baudelaire* (Horizon, 1949).
1947.	*Réflexions sur la question juive,* ed. Paul Morihien (Gallimard). *Anti-Semite and Jew* (Schocken, 1948).
1948.	*Situations* II (Gallimard). Contains articles published in *Qu'est-ce que la littérature?*
1948.	*Qu'est-ce que la littérature?* (Gallimard). *What Is Literature?* (Philosophical Library, 1947).

1948.   *Visages* (Seghers).

1948.   *Situations* III (Gallimard). Selections in *Literary and Philosophical Essays* (Philosophical Library, 1957).

1949.   *Entretiens sur la politique* [in collaboration with David Rousset and Gérard Rosenthal] (Gallimard).

1952.   *Saint-Genêt, comédien et martyr* (Gallimard).

II. SIGNIFICANT ARTICLES BY SARTRE

Most of the articles published by Sartre in *N.R.F.* (1938-1949), in *Cahiers du Sud* (1943-1944), in *Europe* (1939), in *Poésie 44* (1944), in *Figaro* (1945), and in *Les Temps Modernes* beginning in 1946, have been republished in three volumes, *Situations* I, II, and III. Below are listed only those that have not been republished.

"L'Ange du morbide," *Revue sans titre* (1923).

"Légende de la vérité," *Bifur* (1931).

"La Structure intentionnelle de l'image," *Revue de Métaphysique et de Morale* (September, 1938).

"Discussion sur le péché," *Dieu Vivant* IV.

"Introduction aux Ecrits intimes de Baudelaire," *Confluences* (January-February, 1945).

"Présence noire," *Présence Africaine* (Paris-Dakar, November-December, 1947).

"Les communistes et la paix," *Les Temps Modernes*: I (July, 1952); II (October-November, 1952); III (August, 1954).

"Réponse à Albert Camus," *Les Temps Modernes* (August, 1952).

"Réponse à Claude Lefort [on Marxism]," *Les Temps Modernes* (April, 1953).

"Les peintures de Giacometti," *Les Temps Modernes* (June, 1954).

"Le colonialisme est un système," *Les Temps Modernes* (March-April, 1956).

"Sur les événements de Hongrie," *L'Express* (9 November 1956).

"Le fantôme de Staline," *Les Temps Modernes* (January 1957).

"Vous êtes formidables," *Les Temps Modernes* (May 1957).

"Le séquestré de Venise" [on Tintoretto], *Les Temps Modernes* (November, 1957).

"Nous sommes tous des assassins," *Les Temps Modernes* (March, 1958).

III. WORKS DEVOTED TO THE WRITINGS
OF JEAN-PAUL SARTRE

Robert Campbell. *Jean-Paul Sartre ou une littérature philosophique* (Editions Pierre Ardent, 1945).

D. Troisfontaines. *Le Choix de J.-P. Sartre* (Aubier, 1945).

Pierre Boutang and Jean Pingaud. *Sartre est-il un possédé?* (La Table Ronde, 1946).

Francis Jeanson. *Le Problème moral et la pensée de Jean-Paul Sartre* (Editions du Myrte, 1947).

Marc Beigbeder. *L'Homme Sartre* (Bordas, 1947).

Jean Kanapa. *L'Existentialisme n'est pas un humanisme* (Editions Sociales, 1947).

Jean-Marie Grévillot. *Les Grands Courants de la pensée contemporaine* (Beauchesne, 1948).

Gilbert Varet. *L'ontologie de Sartre* (Presses Universitaires, 1948).

P.-H. Simon. *L'homme en procès* (Neuchâtel: La Baconnière, 1950).

Régis Jolivet. *Le problème de la mort chez Heidegger et chez Sartre* (Ed. de Fontenelle, 1950).

Pierre de Boisdeffre. *Métamorphoses de la littérature* (Editions Alsatia, 1951) II, pp. 209-307.

Pierre de Boisdeffre. *Des Vivants et des Morts* (Editions Universitaires, 1954).

Charles Moeller. *Litterature du XXᵉ siècle* (Albin Michel, 1955).

Cahiers de la Compagnie Madeleine–Jean-Louis Barrault XIII. *Connaissance de Sartre* (Julliard, 1955).

Francis Jeanson. *Sartre par lui-même* (Editions du Seuil, 1956).

IV. SIGNIFICANT ARTICLES ON THE WRITINGS OF JEAN-PAUL SARTRE

(Only a few of the most important articles are listed.)

Marcel Arland. "Compte rendu de la Nausée," *N.R.F.* (1 July 1938).

Maurice Merleau-Ponty. "Compte rendu des Mouches," *Confluences* XXV (September-October, 1943).

Gaëtan Picon. "Jean-Paul Sartre et le roman contemporain," *Confluences VIII* (October, 1945).

Maurice Blanchot. "Les Romans de Sartre," *L'Arche* X (October, 1945).

Gabriel Marcel. "Les Chemins de la liberté," *La Nef* XIII (December, 1945).

Jean-José Marchand. "Sartre et les Temps Modernes," *Le Magasin du Spectacle* I (April, 1946).

Claude Cuénot. "Littérature et philosophie chez J.-P. Sartre," *Renaissances* XXI (May, 1946).

Raymond Polin. "Introduction à la philosophie de J.-P. Sartre," *Revue de Paris* XLV (1946).

Claude Roy. "Descriptions critiques," *Poésie* XXXVIII (1947).

Georges Blin. "Jean-Paul Sartre et Baudelaire," *Fontaine* LIX (1947).

Thierry Maulnier. "Jean-Paul Sartre et le suicide de la littérature," *La Table Ronde* II (February, 1948).

André Blanchet. "Comment Jean-Paul Sartre se représente le Diable et le Bon Dieu," *Etudes* (September, 1951).

Claude Lefort. "Le marxisme et Sartre," *Les Temps Modernes* (April, 1953).

"Interview par Henri Magnan," *Le Monde* (1 July 1955).

Maurice Nadeau. "Sartre et l'affaire Hervé," *Les Lettres Nouvelles* (April, 1956).